Page 146 Moss Your City

Page 77 Pastificio Lu

Page 94 Omega Garden

Page 136 Insect Hotel

Page 193 Bouquet IX

Page 110 Nature vs. Technology
Page 216 Living Wall Installation

Page 191 Vintage Plant Shop

Page 121 Shinjuku Gardens

Page 200 Paranoid Bush

Page 172 String Gardens

Page 152 UK Pavilion at the 2010 Shanghai Expo

Page 224 Mobile Garden

MY GREEN CITY

Back to Nature with Attitude and Style

gestalten

The Union Street Urban Orchard
Photo: Mike Massaro

The Union Street Urban Orchard

Following the London Festival of Architecture and lasting through fall, the site of 100 Union Street was transformed into an urban orchard and community garden. Designed by Heather Ring of the Wayward Plant Registry for The Architecture Foundation and built with the help of Bankside Open Spaces Trust and an array of other helpful volunteers, the garden regenerated a disused site in Bankside and created a place for exchange between local residents and visitors to the festival.

The Urban Orchard was also home to the Living-ARK, a zero-carbon pod, which was inhabited during the period of the project to showcase sustainable ways of living. In September 2010 the garden was dismantled and all trees were given to local estates and other community gardens to remain as a lasting legacy of the 2010 London Festival of Architecture.

Photos: Mike Massaro

0800
781 4903

Allotment

PRINZESSINNEN-GÄRTEN

Photos: Marco Clausen

Non-profit company Nomadisch Grün launched community garden Prinzessinnengärten as a pilot project in the summer of 2009. For over half a century, the site at Moritzplatz in Berlin Kreuzberg had been a wasteland, once hidden in the shadows of the Berlin Wall. Along with friends, fans, activists, and neighbors, the group cleared away garbage, built transportable organic vegetable plots, and reaped the first fruits of their labor. Conceived as a place for learning, Prinzessinnengärten has become a place where locals get together to experiment and discover more about organic food production, biodiversity, and climate protection. Herbs and vegetables are grown in raised compost beds without using any pesticides or artificial fertilizers. The project aims to increase biological, social, and cultural diversity in the neighborhood and pioneer a new way of living together in the city. The site in which the community garden momentarily resides is only leased, which induced the team of Nomadisch Grün to create a mobile farm that can easily be packed up and moved to the next unused building site, parking lot or roof.

Motörhead
Oranienstraße
MÄRKISCHES
MÄRKISCHES

Haltbare
fettarme
Milch
1,5%

Vacant Lot

What if: projects have been mapping vacant and neglected spaces that surround inner city housing estates in London. Gaps within the urban fabric both detach and isolate communities. The team has been developing a strategy for how these unloved spaces could be appropriated to accommodate the needs of the local population. The basic need for food and outside space for socializing and recreation was developed into a proposal to transform formerly fenced off and neglected pieces of land into allotment gardens. The first Vacant Lot allotment garden was established in Shoreditch, London in May 2007.

Photos: What if: projects Ltd.

Levitt Goodman Architects

Welcome Hut at the Evergreen Brick Works

Evergreen Brick Works is a national charity in Canada that makes cities more livable. To greet visitors in the months before the official opening of the 12-acre community environmental center, Levitt Goodman Architects were commissioned to build a temporary Welcome Hut. The 98-square-feet hut is designed to provide an immediate node for visitors and to support the Evergreen's mission to showcase for green design and environmentally sustainable initiatives. The hut's primary building materials give new life to refuse: a derelict shipping container was embellished with salvage from the historic backyards including a graffiti door that now leads to a deck, sheets of slate that are now chalkboards, and an electrical panel and factory lamps that now hang from the ceiling as an artful light fixture. Adding to the hut's purpose, a scupper on the roof funnels rainwater into an adjacent rain barrel. After the Welcome Hut was no longer required for its original purpose, it was easily converted into a warming spot and a hot beverage kiosk for skaters in the winter and an information kiosk in the warm months.

Photos: Ben Rahn / A-Frame Inc.

Growing Power

The goal of urban agriculture organization Growing Power is a simple one: to grow food, to grow minds, and to grow community. The Milwaukee-based project started with a farmer, a plot of land, and a core group of dedicated young people. Today, Growing Power transforms communities by supporting people from diverse backgrounds and the environments in which they live through the development of Community Food Systems. These systems provide high-quality, safe, healthy, affordable food for all residents in the community. Growing Power develops Community Food Centers, as a key component of Community Food Systems, through training, active demonstration, outreach, and technical assistance.

1

2

3

Mary Mattingly

The Waterpod

Conceptualized and designed by New York-based Mary Mattingly, The Waterpod is a floating, sculptural eco-habitat designed in the face of rising sea levels and lack of usable land. In 2009, it navigated the waters of New York Harbor on a six-month test journey during which Mattingly and other artists lived on The Waterpod, hosting public events and exhibitions. As a sustainable, navigable living space, The Waterpod serves as a model for creative living possibilities, appropriate technologies, art, and design. The Waterpod structure was built on a deck barge where systems were installed to generate food, water, and energy. Four cabins were built for a group of resident artists along with communal areas for the artists and visitors. The Waterpod was to be a free and participatory public space in the waterways of New York City, and represents an intervention and a gift from a team of artists, designers, builders, engineers, activists working with various groups, as well as companies participating "pro bono publico" or "for the public good." These contributors were brought together to create an environment that included public resources and a private experiment, an aquatic and terrestrial, interior and exterior, mobile hybrid. The platform moved through all the five boroughs of New York and Governors Island between June and October 2009. In addition to the team that conducted the project, many artists from New York and elsewhere came to visit and contribute to its evolution.

Images:
1 Waterpod 3D Design by Lux Visual Effects;
2-4 Mary Mattingly

4

1

2

3

4

Landschaftspark Duisburg-Nord

With some 100 projects, the International Building Exhibition (IBA) Emscher Park in the Ruhr District in Germany set the goal of developing and ecologically renewing the highly contaminated former industrial and coal mining area. The Duisburg-Nord Landscape Park is one of these projects: The existing patterns and fragments formed by industrial use were taken, developed, and re-interpreted with a new syntax and interlaced into a new landscape.

Photos:
1, 4 © Siegfried Dammrath;
2 Manfred Kortmann;
3 © Markus van Offern

WORK Architecture Company

Public Farm 1

Public Farm 1 (P.F.1) was a project designed by WORK Architecture Company for MoMA and P.S.1's Young Architects Program in order to provide an outdoor social space for summer 2008. By combining playful programs with educational ones, P.F.1's intention was to create a sense of community around the shared experience of growing food. The structure was built entirely from recyclable materials, it was 100 % solar-powered and used rain collection for irrigation. The cardboard tubes held planters for vegetables, herbs, and fruit.

Photos: Elizabeth Felicella

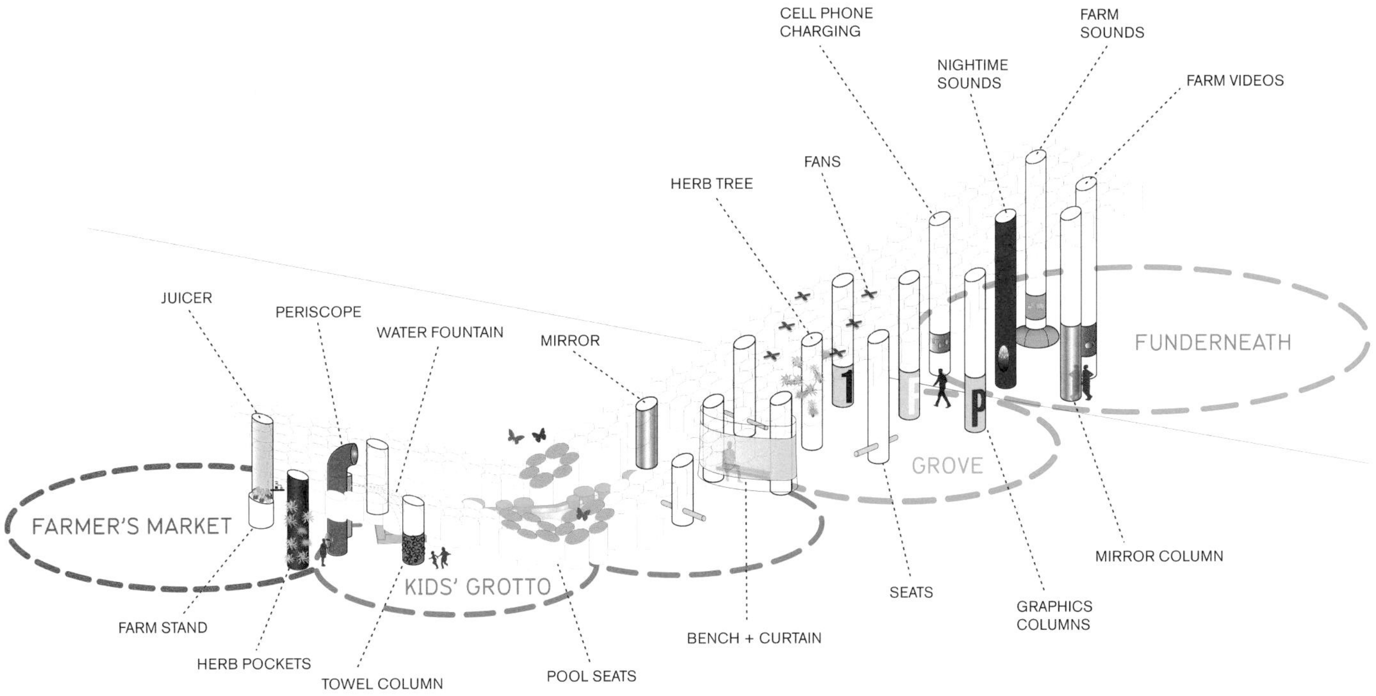

CELL PHONE CHARGING
FARM SOUNDS
NIGHTIME SOUNDS
FARM VIDEOS
FANS
HERB TREE
JUICER
PERISCOPE
WATER FOUNTAIN
MIRROR
FUNDERNEATH
GROVE
FARMER'S MARKET
KIDS' GROTTO
MIRROR COLUMN
SEATS
GRAPHICS COLUMNS
FARM STAND
BENCH + CURTAIN
HERB POCKETS
TOWEL COLUMN
POOL SEATS

WORK Architecture Company
Public Farm 1
Photo: Elizabeth Felicella

Ernst van der Hoeven & Frank Bruggeman

Dahlia Drive

At the invitation of MU, Flux/S, and housing cooperative Woonbedrijf, artist Frank Bruggeman and landscape architect Ernst van der Hoeven conceived Dahlia Drive: a garden strip lying alongside one of the sandy avenues around Dutch electronics corporation Philips' former NatLab building. Here, 50 different varieties of dahlia, from Honkas to Caribbean Delights and from Stolze von Berlin to Chat Noirs, flourished between July and November 2009. Amid the violence of excavators, bulldozers, and building material but tended with loving care, these vulnerable flowers gradually conquered Strijp-S district. Dahlia Drive was not just any old dahlia garden: it was rather a tiny oasis, a labyrinth of circling footpaths for visitors to stroll among the various dahlia borders. Because however gray and rough this Strijp-S building site is now, ultimately these are grounds meant for people and for nature. And according to Bruggeman and Van der Hoeven, nature does not have to be neatly raked to be convincingly beautiful. With the help of redundant building material and devoted voluntary gardeners, a plot of land can be given an identity and a face of its own.

Photos: Ernst van der Hoeven

1

Arup

Zuidas Corn Field

Zuidas (literally “Southern Axis”) is a major development zone in Amsterdam. Part of the development strategy is to involve the interaction of complex, sometime contradictory components to ensure that the place has a richness and authenticity of experience. In this context, the Zuidas Development in Amsterdam in conjunction with the master planning team of Arup and DRO started a temporary urban farming pilot project in some of the most prominent empty plots in Amsterdam. Aiming to provide a specific character and to influence the way the development is perceived by the local community, this new urban agricultural garden explores the notion of local food supply, new types of public realm and raises awareness of urban farming and localized food production.

Photos:
1 Janus van den Eijnden;
2 Juan-Mei Hu

2

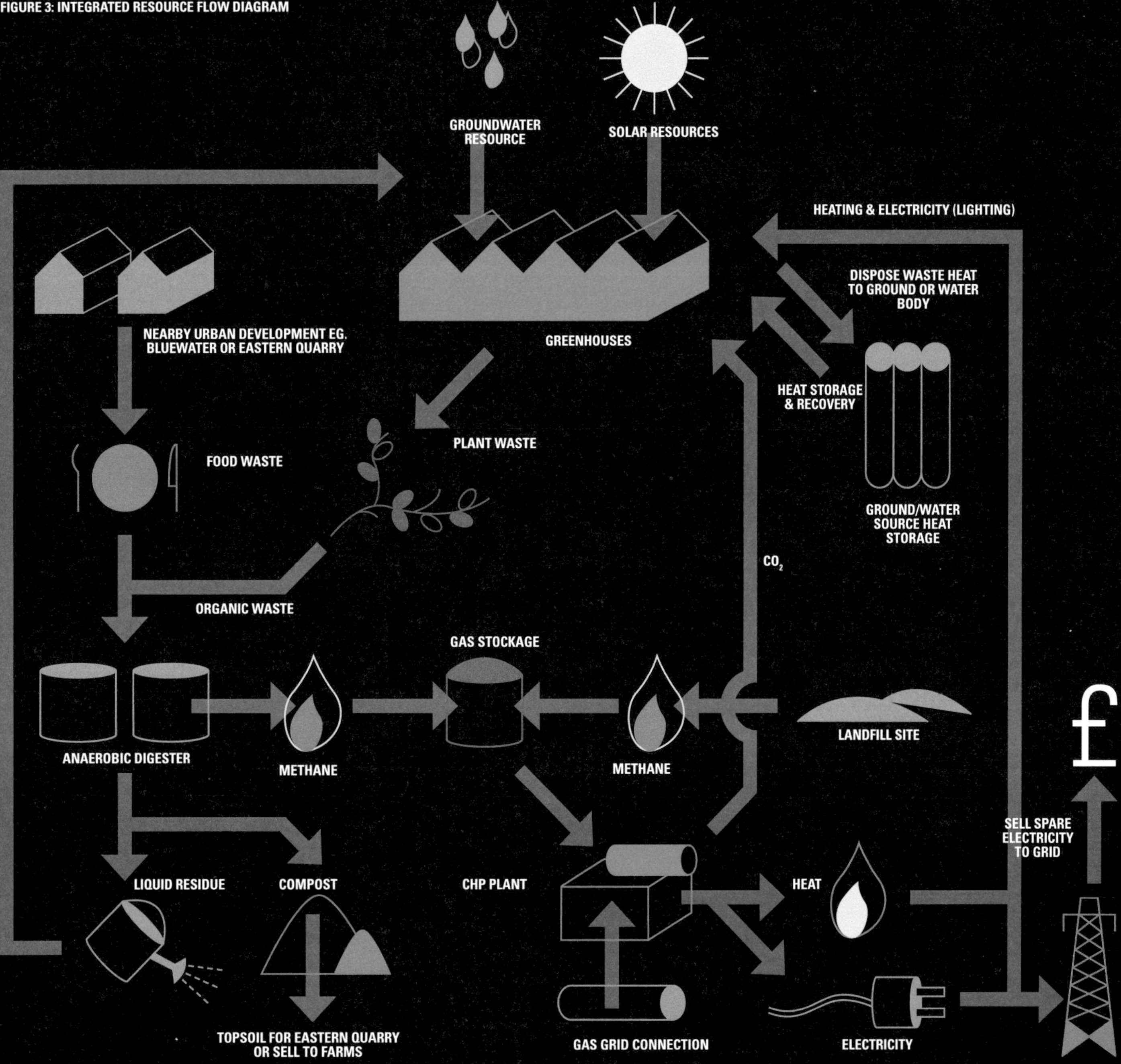

FIGURE 3: INTEGRATED RESOURCE FLOW DIAGRAM

Arup Temporal Land Use Strategy

Responding to the requirement of generating revenue from landholdings until market realities allow the proposed mixed-use masterplan to be implemented, Arup developed the vision for s short to midterm utilisation of land awaiting development for intensive, high yield agriculture. The proposal responds to the pressing issue of rising food prices and the growing need for the localization of sustainable living environments, and identifies the business relationships that are key to the successful delivery of the project. The option of greenhouse-based, intensive agriculture on this site has been chosen as it allows for a quick implementation, while simultaneously taking full advantage of the site opportunities and minimizing near-term expenditure on bulk earth works or infrastructure.

CibicWorkshop

Rethinking Happiness: A Campus in the Fields & Rural Urbanism

Rethinking Happiness is a research project led by Aldo Cibic on new possible communities.

A Campus in the Fields, planned in the Venetian lagoon, is a concept based on nutritional and energy self-sufficiency: agriculture, vegetable gardens, tourism, and technology can thus coexist in the same environment.

Rural Urbanism is a concept planned for a large rural territory one hour from Shanghai with an ancient agricultural tradition that is crushed between a growing industrial zone and a new city. The idea is to create an agricultural park of four square kilometers inhabited by 8,000 people with low-density residential structures, preserving the agriculture and offering green spaces for the inhabitants. The project calls for a group of elevated buildings on the streets, to create a perpendicular grid that floats over the countryside. In the middle of this "agricultural central park" there are specialized farms that produce crops for the sustainable, profitable development of the countryside. The challenge is to create a new community with shared services, and new activities and relationships, in tune with the territory.

Photos: Matteo Cibic;
opposite page Chuck Felton

Marcello Fantuz
Urban Tomato
above Food Cooperative for the Neighborhood
In a residential area of Havana, Cuba, citizens set up and organized the cooperative that takes care of this plot. The food produced is consumed by the habitants of the neighborhood.

Productive Urban Code
Map illustrating the potentials of the unbuilt space inbetween the residential houses of the district Vedado in Havana.

Maaike Bertens
Kavelkleed
Carpet inspired by the typical Dutch polder landscape.

1

2

3

atelier le balto

Landscape architecture studio atelier le balto from Berlin transforms seemingly neglected urban spaces into unique installations. Transformation processes and transience always inspire its gardens and public spaces, which are atmospheric rather than scenic. Since the founding of the studio in 2001 atelier le balto has created gardens all over Europe.

1-3 Woistdergarten?– Tafel-Garten
Temporary garden at the Hamburger Bahnhof contemporary art museum in Berlin.

4, 5 Cage d'Amour
Plant installation at Schauspiel Frankfurt theater.

6 Jardin Sauvage
Garden at the Palais de Tokyo in Paris.

Photos:
1-4 atelier le balto
5 Frank Kraus
6 Yann Monel

4

5

Coloco

La Plage, Mirage à Beaudésert

Community garden in Beaudésert (Mérignac), France.

1

2

3

1 Anne Hamersky
In her Southside Chicago back-yard, Carolyn Thomas' grandson stands with the fresh garlic they grew.
Photo: Anne Hamersky

3 Andrew Buurman
Allotments
Photo: © VG Bild-Kunst, Bonn 2010

2 Stedelijk Museum Amsterdam, Marjetica Potrc, Wilde Westen
The Cook, the Farmer, His Wife and Their Neighbor
Participatory project in Amsterdam New West.
Photo: Gert Jan van Rooij

Itay Laniado

Garden Tools

For this project Israeli designer Itay Laniado approached the topic of garden tools, investigating material, aesthetic, and function. The bulk of the research focused on the development of a technique of bending and stretching wood into functional forms while maintaining the simplicity both of the production process and of the functional approach to the tools. Laniado is a graduate of the Industrial Design department at Bezalel Academy of Arts and Design in Jerusalem.

Photo: Oded Antman

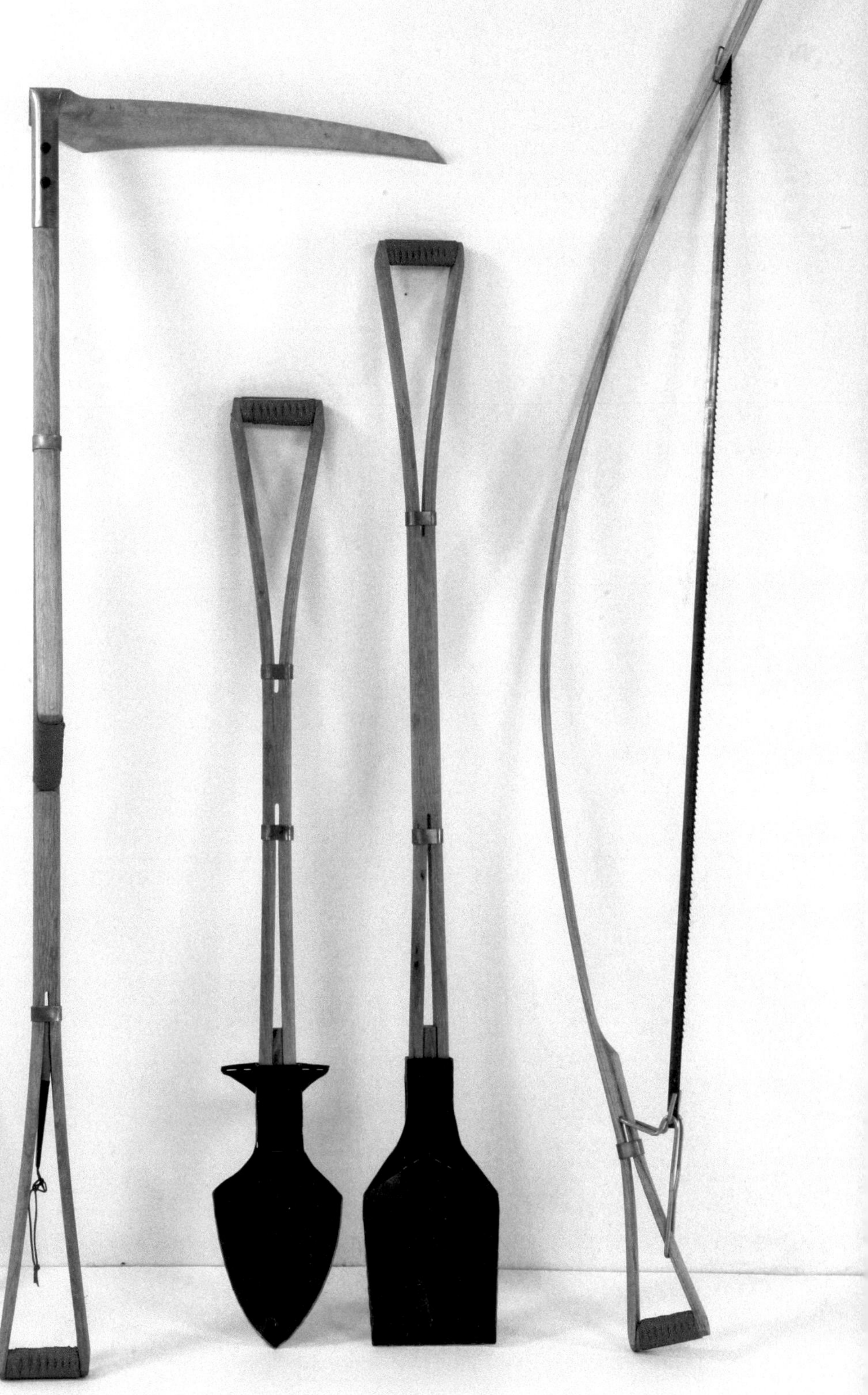

Victory Gardens

Victory Gardens 2008+ was a pilot project funded by the City of San Francisco to support the transition of backyard, front yard, window boxes, rooftops, and unused land into organic food production areas. The SF Victory Garden project built on the successful Victory Garden programs of the First and Second World Wars, where fruit, vegetable, and herb gardens were planted to reduce the pressure on the public food supply. Today, the fight is against an unhealthy, impersonal, and ineffective food system. The victory is growing food at home for increased local food security and reducing the food miles associated with the average American meal. In 2008 the organization chose 15 households that represented the diversity of San Francisco to participate in the program. Candidates were chosen regardless of income, ethnicity, available space, neighborhood, gardening experience, or lifestyle. The organization's staff installed and supported each Victory Garden; participation in the pilot program included a yearlong commitment and a specified number of Victory Garden tour dates. Aim of the project was to create a community of urban food producers and the collection of data on the location and productive potential of urban land through the program's City Garden Registry.

Photos: Amy Franceschini

Pam & Jenny
Euralille – Parc des Dondaines
Illustrations for construction fences of a future public park in Lille.
Photo: Nathalie Pollet

FUTUREFARMERS

1 Rainwater Harvester/ Gray-water System Feedback Loop
A water saving system made from salvaged materials. It stores two types of water—water that normally runs down the drain as the water gets hot and rainwater. The water is stored in the three small recycling bins, which can also be used as benches to sit on. The hand crank device on the right is used to pump stored water back to the sink to be used at a later time. The sink is equipped with a variable drain allowing the user to decide whether the water runs back into the storage units, into the gray-water system to the garden or out to the municipal sewage system.

Futurefarmers is a group of artists and designers working together since 1995. Their design studio serves as a platform to support art projects, artist in residency programs, and research interests. The members of Futurefarmers are teachers, researchers, designers, gardeners, scientists, engineers, illustrators, people who know how to sew, cooks, and bus drivers with a common interest in creating work that challenges current social, political, and economic systems. Through their work, Futurefarmers have become innovators within the new media art and design contexts. They have exhibited internationally at numerous galleries and museums, including the New York Museum of Modern Art, the Whitney Biennial and the ZKM in Karlsruhe, Germany.

Photos: Amy Franceschini

1

2

3

4

2, 3 Nearest Nature
Nearest Nature was a three day workshop and exhibition within the Urban Concerns project at the Bildmuseet in Umeå, Sweden. In collaboration with local botanists, Academy of Fine Arts students, and the general public a body of work was created to respond to the Linnaean system of taxonomy, knowledge of local flora, and its inference on the effects of globalization on the local environment.

4 The Reverse Ark: Headlands Kitchen Garden
The Reverse Ark was commissioned by the Headlands Center for the Arts in Sausalito, California. Twenty-four different herbs were chosen by a chef to be planted. The garden design had to adhere to very strict National Park criteria; therefore a covered boat garden was built to protect the herbs from deer and mountain lions. The Art Center is located less than a mile from the rising Pacific Ocean so the garden will be able to float away if the tides continue to rise. Over 100 guests inaugurated the garden by hand planting the individual plants.

Doors of Perception **City Eco Lab**

City Eco Lab was a two-week festival that took place in St Etienne, France in 2008. More than 50 projects involved productive urban gardens, low energy food storage, communal composting solutions, re-discovery of hidden rivers, neighborhood energy dashboards, de-motorized courier services, and a wide variety of software tools to help people share resources.

Virginia Echeverria Whipple
Untitled
Photograph, magazine cut ups and colored paper.

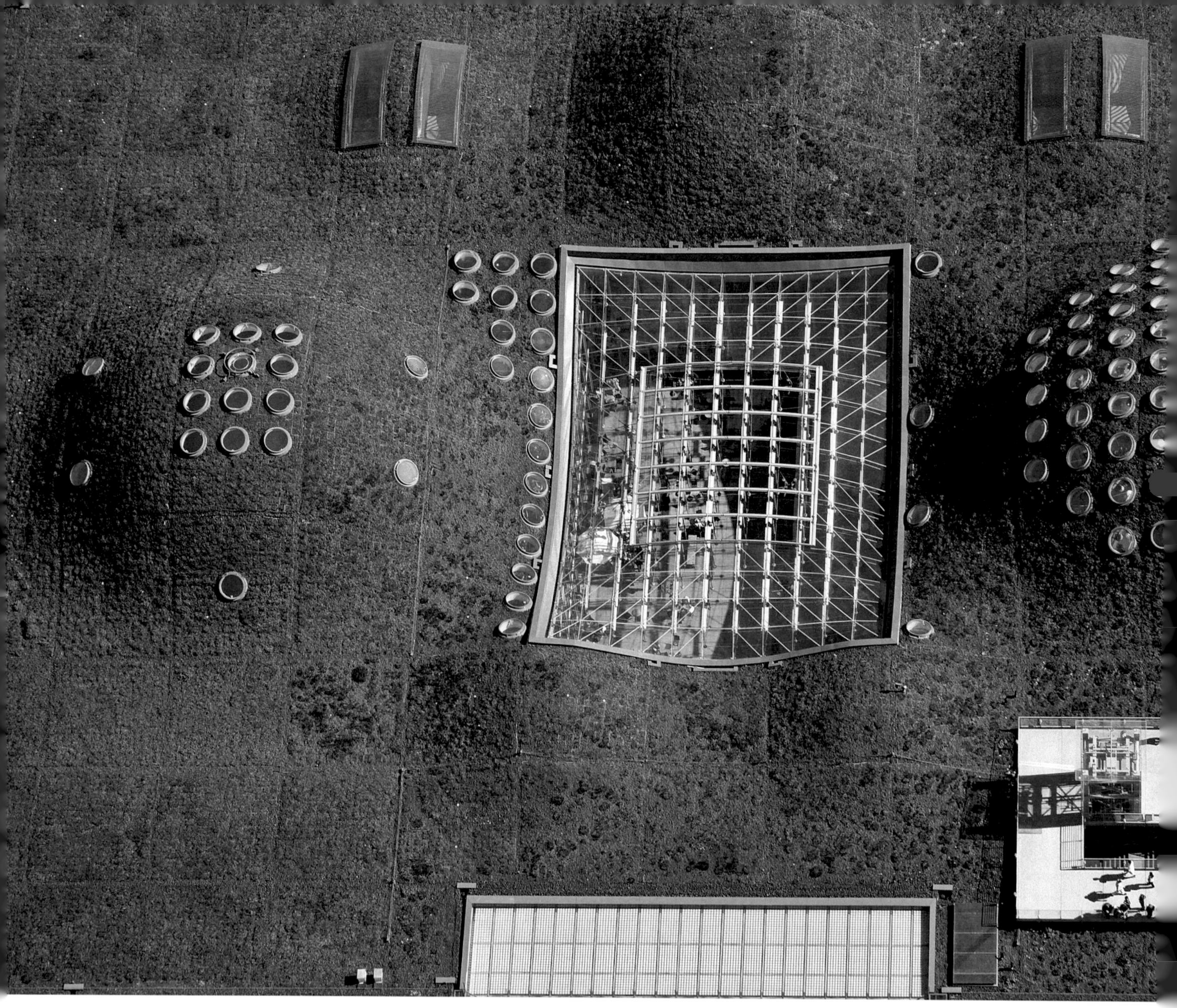

2

3

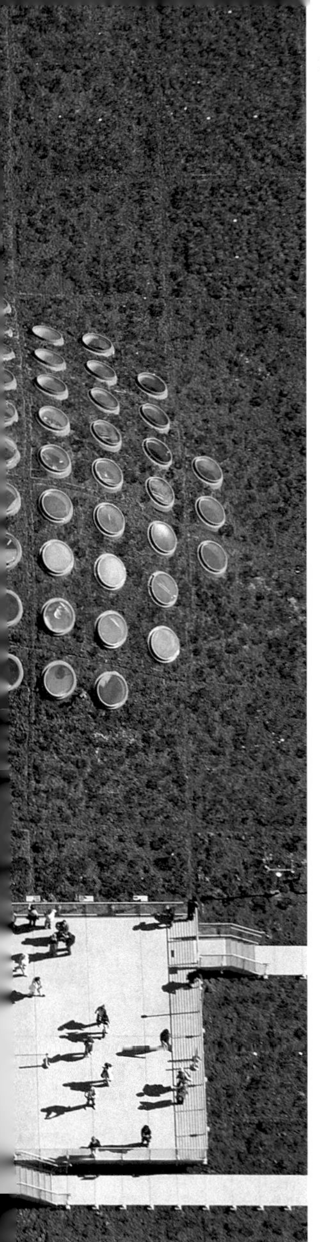

1

4

5

Renzo Piano
California Academy of Sciences
The undulating roof of the new California Academy of Sciences building designed by Renzo Piano is landscaped with native plant species which are drought resistant and do not require irrigation. The 2.5-acre green roof extends beyond the perimeter walls and becomes a glass canopy providing shade, protection from the rain, and generating energy through more than 55,000 photovoltaic cells in the glass. In the center of the roof a glazed skylight covers a piazza. Much smaller skylights distributed over the surface of the roof allow natural light into the exhibition space and can be opened automatically for natural ventilation of the space below.
Photos:
1, 5 Tom Fox, © SWA Group;
2 Ishida Shunji © Rpbw, Renzo Piano Building Workshop;
3 Nic Lehoux © Rpbw;
4 Justine Lee © Rpbw

Durante Kreuk
Parcel 6 Rooftop Garden
Green roofs, Olympic Village,
Vancouver.
Photos: DK

Levitt Goodman Architects
Native Child and Family Services of Toronto

The new **Native Child and Family Services of Toronto** (NCFST) consolidate social and culture-based services for aboriginal children and families within a 30,000-square-feet office building in the heart of downtown Toronto. **Levitt Goodman Architects** were assigned to create a place that would reconnect urban aboriginals with nature in the heart of the city and to project a bold visual presence for the First Nations community. Opened in June 2010, the former 1980s office building now houses a drop-in childcare center, an aboriginal artist studio, family, mental health, social services, and administration offices as well as a contemporary iteration of a longhouse and a rooftop healing lodge and fire circle surrounded by a lush roof garden.
Photos: Ben Rahn / A-Frame

Hoerr Schaudt Landscape Architects

Gary Comer Youth Center Green Roof

This vegetable green roof garden designed as an outdoor classroom adds an unusual dimension to traditional green roof design. A full-time gardener utilizes a planting system custom-designed by Hoerr Schaudt **to teach inner-city youth methods in gardening. The garden maximizes two heat sources, ambient heat from the building and solar energy, which allows for gardening nearly all year. Soil depths of nearly a foot allow for a wide variety of plant material.**

Photos: Scott Shigley;
opposite page Okrent Associates

Brooklyn Grange

As a commercial organic farming business located on New York City rooftops, Brooklyn Grange grows vegetables in the city and sells them to local people and businesses. The company's goal is to improve access to healthy food, to connect city people more closely to farms and food production, and to make urban farming a viable enterprise and livelihood. Although functioning as a privately owned and operated enterprise, Brooklyn Grange is community oriented and open to the public. School groups, families, and volunteers are welcome to visit, participate, and learn.

Photo: Brooklyn Grange

Carrier

1

2

1, 2 Ginza Farm
Omotesandō Farm
Rooftop farm in Omotesandō, Tokyo.
Photos: Ginza Farm Corp.

3 NUTZDACH
Swiss organization NUTZDACH promotes vegetable and herb gardens on roofs of residential buildings.
Photo: Brigitte Fässler

3

Eve Mosher

Seeding the City

Eve Mosher is an artist and interventionist living and working in New York City. Her works use investigations of the landscape as starting points for audience exploration of urban issues. Her public works raise issues of involvement in the environment, public/private space use, history of place, cultural and social issues, and our own understanding of the urban ecosystem. Seeding the City, an environmentally conscious pyramid scheme, simultaneously promotes community building and addresses urban environmental issues by inviting the public to enlist fellow neighbors to join a network of Green Roof Modules. These modules remove heat from the surrounding air and roof surface through evapotranspiration, the process of using heat to evaporate water through plant leaves and soil. In addition to decreasing heat island effect, green roofs foster inner-city ecosystems, filter gray-water, lower heat stress, and reduce energy use, air pollution, and greenhouse gas emissions. Once installed, the modules are marked with a flag and street level signage to draw more attention to this network, which is virtually mapped and tracked for its impact on local heat island effect online.

1

3

4

1, 2 ANNE GABRIEL-JÜRGENS PHOTOGRAPHY
Urban Farming, NYC

3, 4 Ben Faga **Rough Luxe Hives**

Looking into local, sustainable methods of producing his own food and food for others, Ben Faga started beekeeping to explore his interest in alternative ways of sourcing food within an urban community. Currently he has two biodynamic apiaries in London, one at the Rough Luxe Hotel in Kings Cross where he keeps three hives and one on his studio's roof in Dalston where he has two hives. Through his work, Faga has become increasingly aware of the dire situation of honeybees. His take on the vanishing of the bees not only lies in large-scale agrochemical practices, but also in modern beekeeping methods. The modern beekeeper forces bees to draw out comb one millimeter larger than they would naturally. This leads to stressed hives of large bees that are much more susceptible to disease and mite infestation. Keeping the bees in line with biodynamic standards allows the bees to draw out comb according to their needs. Using this method, he has few problems with disease and mites, unlike some of his colleagues.

Photos: Ben Faga

Brooklyn Brine

After being laid off from his job as a chef, Shamus Jones joined forces with his friend Josh Egnew and together they launched their indie pickle enterprise Brooklyn Brine. The award-winning pickles are made from locally grown, organic produce and are hand packed. Their creations like smoked baby carrots, tarragon- and fennel-infused beets, and pattypan squash in a curry-flavored brine are sold at specialty stores throughout New England and can be purchased online.

opposite page

Ryan Rhodes **Johnson's Backyard Garden Corporate Design**

Johnson's Backyard Garden is a 70-acre certified organic farm that functions through a Community Supported Agriculture (CSA) program. Members pay in advance for a share of the upcoming harvest and are ensured produce that is harvested from the farm and delivered to the members' neighborhoods on the same day. For the corporate design, artist Ryan Rhodes used pieces of wood that had been inked and printed.

JOHNSON'S BACKYARD GARDEN

1

FRUIT CITY

2

Photos:
1, 2, 4 Mike Massaro;
3 Vahakn Matossian

Fruit City is a growing map and network of all the fruit trees in public spaces in London, logged and mapped by the Fruit City team and users. Additionally, the website lists associated organizations and programs as well as recipes and uses for fruit. The project's in house designer Vahakn Matossian has developed a series of objects for the urban forager, from picking to juicing, which are also available via Fruit City. The initiative's aim is to remind Londoners that, despite living in a big city, nature is right on their doorstep. The trees of the city grow literally tons of blackberries, mulberries, apples, pears, plums, figs, strawberries, and even some secret kiwis, and a lot of that fruit goes to waste unpicked while huge amounts of fruit are shipped in from all over the world. Beyond providing a map of fruit trees, Fruit City hopes to re-engage urbanites with the wild around them and to get local community orchards planted.

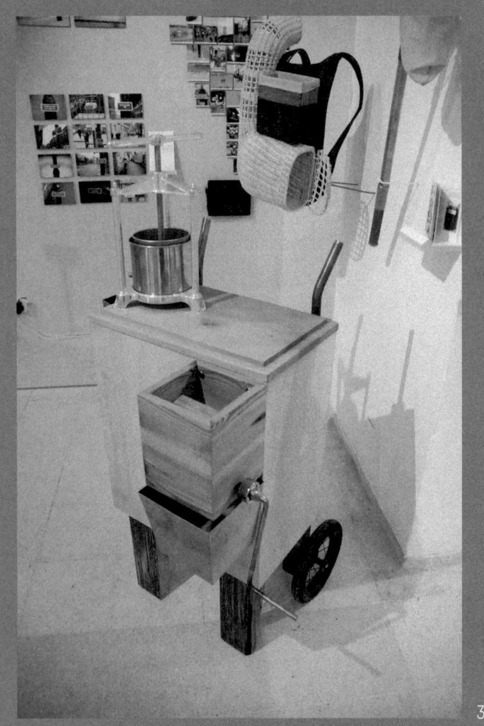

3

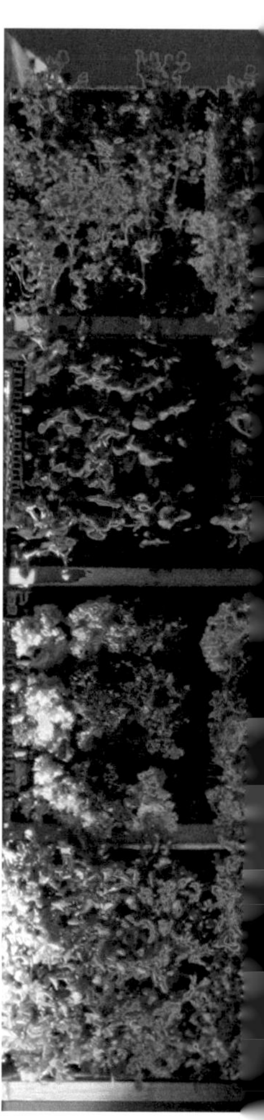

Turf Design **Salad Bar**

The Salad Bar was featured in the 2004 Year of the Built Environment Future Gardens exhibition in the Royal Botanic Gardens, Sydney. The exhibition demonstrated how environmental sustainability could be practically incorporated into contemporary living. In 2005, the project was invited to join the Houses of the Future exhibition at Sydney Olympic Park. The Salad Bar provides a modular vertical growing structure with a smaller footprint than the generic garden enabling it to occupy small spaces with the same square meter surface coverage. Integrating a bar within the vegetated wall provides a playful vision of how self-sufficiency can be incorporated into contemporary urban living. The Salad Bar collects rainwater and stores it in a central reservoir at the base of the wall. It is then reticulated by pumps into a drip irrigation system that feeds into soil pillows within each growing module. Beyond its current form, the Salad Bar can be advanced as an integral part of future urban environments, including residential, commercial, and architectural applications.

Photos: Simon Wood

Mike Meiré for Dornbracht Edges

The Farm Project

"Orchestrated chaos" is how Mike Meiré, designer and art director, calls his farm project, which he conceived within the framework of Dornbracht Edges, a series of projects at the interface between architecture, design, and art. The exhibited kitchen was created as a workshop for the senses and to restore the harmony between man and food. To counterpoint the slick appearance of today's minimal kitchen design Meiré focused on a rather rustic look by choosing the archaic shape of a barn. Pots, pans, and hams were hung from the ceiling. Live sheep, goats, and pigs served as a reminder that meat does not come from the supermarket, but from living animals that have to be slaughtered. As a social event The Farm Project tells stories of life and death, past and present, transience, and honesty. Dornbracht presented The Farm Project by Mike Meiré for the first time at the Milan Furniture Fair in April 2006. Due to its great success, the installation was presented during the Passagen 2007 exhibitions in Cologne, as an associate project at the opening days of the Münster 07 Sculpture Projects and at the ART Basel Miami Beach exhibition in December 2007.

Photos: Tim Giesen

Studio Formafantasma

Autarchy

Autarchy is an installation that proposes an autonomous way of producing goods and outlines a hypothetical scenario where a community embraces a serene and self-inflicted embargo and nature is personally cultivated, harvested, and processed to feed and make tools to serve human necessities. Autarchy pays homage to the uncomplicated, the simple, and the everyday. In the installation, a collection of functional and durable vessels and lamps, naturally desiccated or low temperature baked, are produced with a biomaterial composed of 70 % flour, 20 % agricultural waste, and 10 % natural limestone. The differences in the color palette are obtained by the selection of distinct vegetables, spices, and roots that are dried, boiled, or filtered for their natural dyes. As guests in the project, Studio Formafantasma invited the Italian broom maker Giuseppe Brunello and the renowned French bakery Poilane to participate in developing the installation. The cereal sorgho works as a link between these crafts—in a perfect production process without waste, the cereal is harvested and used to create tools, vessels, and foods. As an open source where information and knowledge are shared, the installation displays the different steps in the research, explaining the material and production processes of the products. The furniture used to display the products is based on the manufacturing and drying processes used in the project and features a drying oven and a mill. Autarchy suggests an alternative way of producing goods where inherited knowledge is used to find sustainable and uncomplicated solutions.

Photos: Studio Formafantasma

Studio Toogood

Corn Craft

Taking inspiration from crafts found in traditional folk culture, Gallery FUMI and creative consultancy Studio Toogood staged a contemporary installation during London Design Festival in 2009 based around the sustainable and natural material, corn. The launch of the exhibition was celebrated with a conceptual dining event based on Harvest Festival, with a corn-based menu designed by The Modern Pantry.

Photos: Tom Mannion

Studio Toogood

Super Natural

Super Natural, a project by Studio Toogood, was dedicated to foraging, collecting, and observing in the English countryside. Visitors were encouraged to experience a mushroom installation by New Forest forager Mrs Tee, while experiencing a bespoke scent dedicated to woodland by Francis Kurkdjian. A feast was prepared by La Fromagerie, who collaborated with Arabeschi di Latte in creating a menu and eating space using seasonal ingredients with an emphasis on foraged foods at the Bramble Café. Toogood launched Assemblage 1, a collection of furniture using three recurring elements—wood, brass, and stone—with an emphasis on English-sourced materials and local craftsmen including stonemasons, carpenters, and metalworkers. The Super Natural project took place during London Design Festival 2010.

Photos: Tom Mannion;
opposite page Arabeschi di Latte

ARABESCHI DI LATTE

Photos: Arabeschi di Latte

Founded in 2001, Arabeschi di Latte is an Italian culinary design collective with a passion for conviviality. The group's mission is to experiment with new design concepts that relate to food and to focus on its fascinating power to create situations and relationships. In the last 10 years, Arabeschi di Latte has created and exhibited a variety of food-related projects and events.

Arabeschi di Latte is based on the idea of creating a daily sense of happiness that is pursued through various strategies of participation and interaction that respond to basic and pleasurable needs in social life.

1 Compost Dinner
The **Compost Dinner** was a completely compostable banquet that examined food in terms of sustainability and "re-use." Everything was recycled as compost: the cardboard table, leaves, newspapers, tableware, and food leftovers. All waste was collected in a big cardboard box and then delivered to a farm. The Compost Dinner is an **Arabeschi di Latte** concept that took part in "Arte & Cibo," a project by Associazione Culurale Modidi and Centro di Riuso Creativa Remida in Codroipo, Italy in 2008.

2-4 BQ Interactive Dinner
The **Big Quality** project was an ironic statement reacting to the quality and quantity of food in western diets: the exaggerated myths surrounding diets and health as well as the extra large portions. The concept was to have a "big feast in a healthy version" consisting of wooden fruit and vegetable crates borrowed from a farmers' market and filled with primary and mostly organic food products. The dinner became an interactive event, as the guests could create simple but intensly flavored Mediterranean dishes using a mortar and pestle or a grater to personalize their plate. The eco-friendly food containers were similar to fast food packaging, available in sizes S, M, L, XL.

3

4

2

1, 2 BQ Interactive Dinner

3, 4 Mia Market
With **Mia Market** the collective opened a self-service restaurant and design shop in Rome that sells local, seasonal produce and groceries.

1

2

3

KM ZERO
"UNA CAROTA
DIAMANTI ROSSI
DEL SOLCO

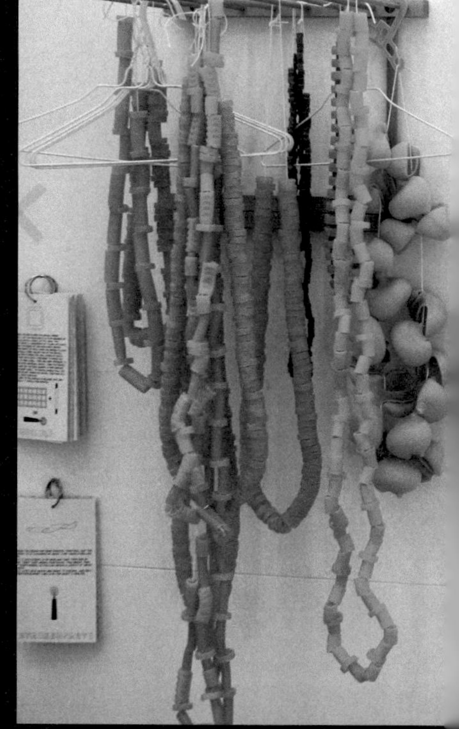
PASTA
DRYER

3

1

POTATO
ARABESCHI
DILATTE
ORG
OF DOUGH 5
CUT THE SNAKE
YEAR
OF
POTATO
INFO→

2

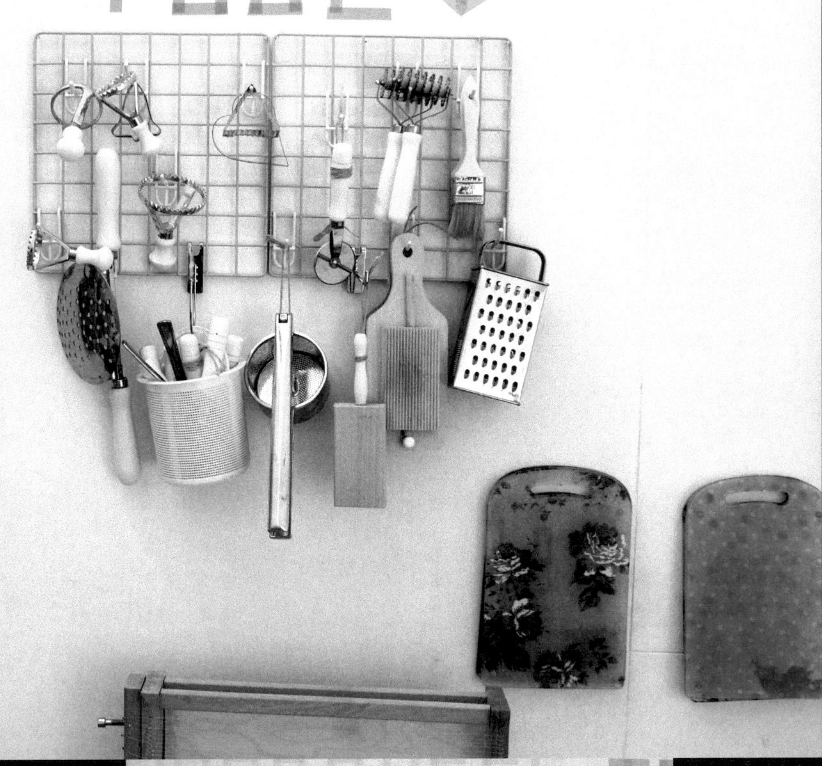

1, 2 Gnocchi Bar
Gnocchi Bar is a touring project where culture, culinary tradition, and manual craft come together to form a special bar in which participants are invited to take an invigorating and enlightening rest.
During London Design Week 2008, **Gnocchi Bar** took place inside the Designersblock venue. Gnocchi based recipes were prepared using traditional tools along a communal table, inviting visitors to join in and enjoy.

3-5 Pastificio Lu
Pastificio Lu is an installation by **Arabeschi di Latte**, functioning as a workshop for people to create their own hand-made pasta. Incorporating the sense of touch, the workshop aimed to highlight the important interplay between simple ingredients and their creative interpretation.
Pastificio Lu was part of the Tokyo Designtide extension in 2009.

4

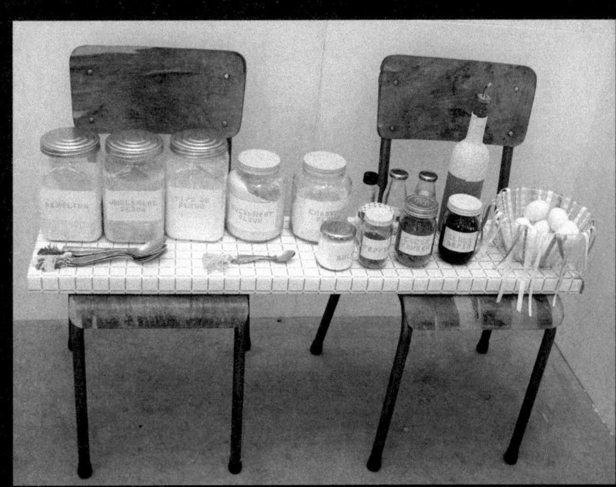

5

Riverside Picnic
Beach party picnic on the bank of Florence's Arno river for the San Giovanni fireworks spectacle.

UP Projects

Mobile Picnic Pavillion

The Mobile Picnic Pavilion is a mobile vegetable garden created by performance artist Francis Thorburn that travelled around Islington's streets during the summer of 2010. Pulled by a merry band of performing gardeners, the Mobile Picnic Pavillion provided opportunities for passers-by to explore the portable green space and picnic upon it. The garden vehicle draws on the principles of a sustainable lifestyle while adopting the sentiments of social sculpture and the potential for green spaces as places for social exchange. With his vegetable garden housed in a greenhouse-inspired structure, Thorburn developed a two-phase performative element for the viewer: an encounter on the roadways as Thorburn and his performers navigate the human-powered garden vehicle through the streets; and a participatory experience as the vehicle parks and folds out to become a picnic area for members of the public to eat their sandwiches on and engage with the artwork. The Mobile Picnic Pavilion was produced by UP Projects as part of the Secret Garden Project, a pan-London program of temporary commissions and pop up art events in secret gardens and lesser known green spaces.

Photos: Courtesy of UP Projects

Maaike Bertens

Public Pie

Public Pie is a mobile kitchen that caters to the senses while creating an intimate atmosphere in public. The oven not only heats up the pies but also serves as a little bench for comfortable outdoor sitting.

Photos:
1 Claudia Castaldi;
2 Eduardo Costa

1

2

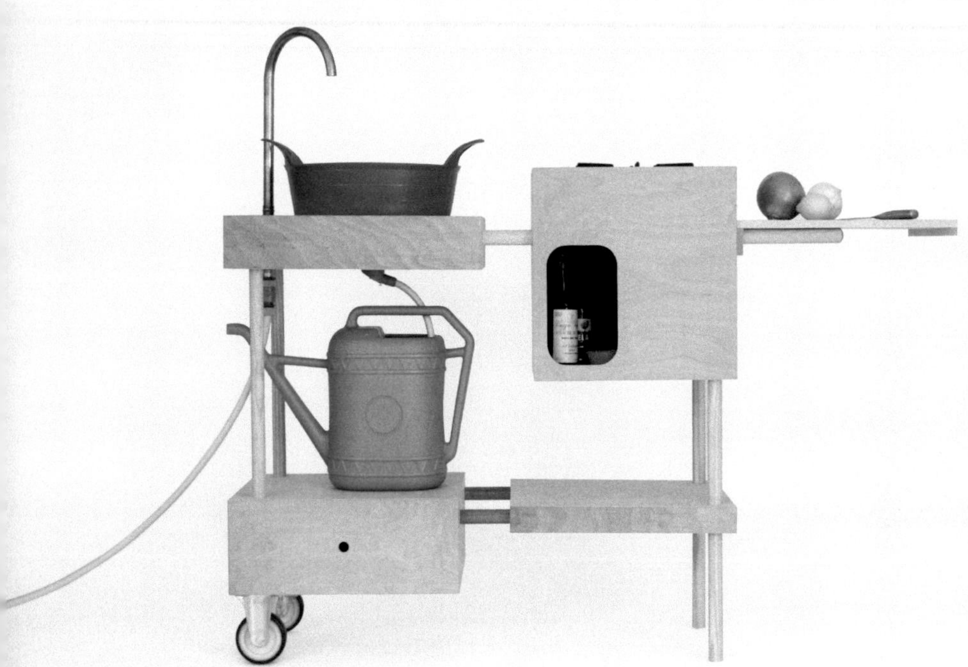

1

1 Studiomama

The Mobile Outdoor Kitchen

The Mobile Outdoor Kitchen comprises a gas cooking hob, a bucket sink, a chopping board, and storage for tableware, utensils, and a few food ingredients. Water is connected from a garden hose and wastewater is collected in a watering can beneath the sink, so gray-water can be reused.

2 Lisa Johansson

Compost Distiller

The Compost Distiller is a system in which plant based kitchen waste gets processed into alcohol, soil nutrients, and compost. The design is mainly suitable for communal applications such as kitchens, cafés, and restaurants, or as a shared facility between neighbors. The same system can be developed for both smaller or larger scale applications. With the Compost Distiller, product designer Lisa Johansson intended to create a product which fully utilizes the estimated 38 percent of organic content in domestic waste such as fruit and vegetable peelings produced annually in the UK.

2

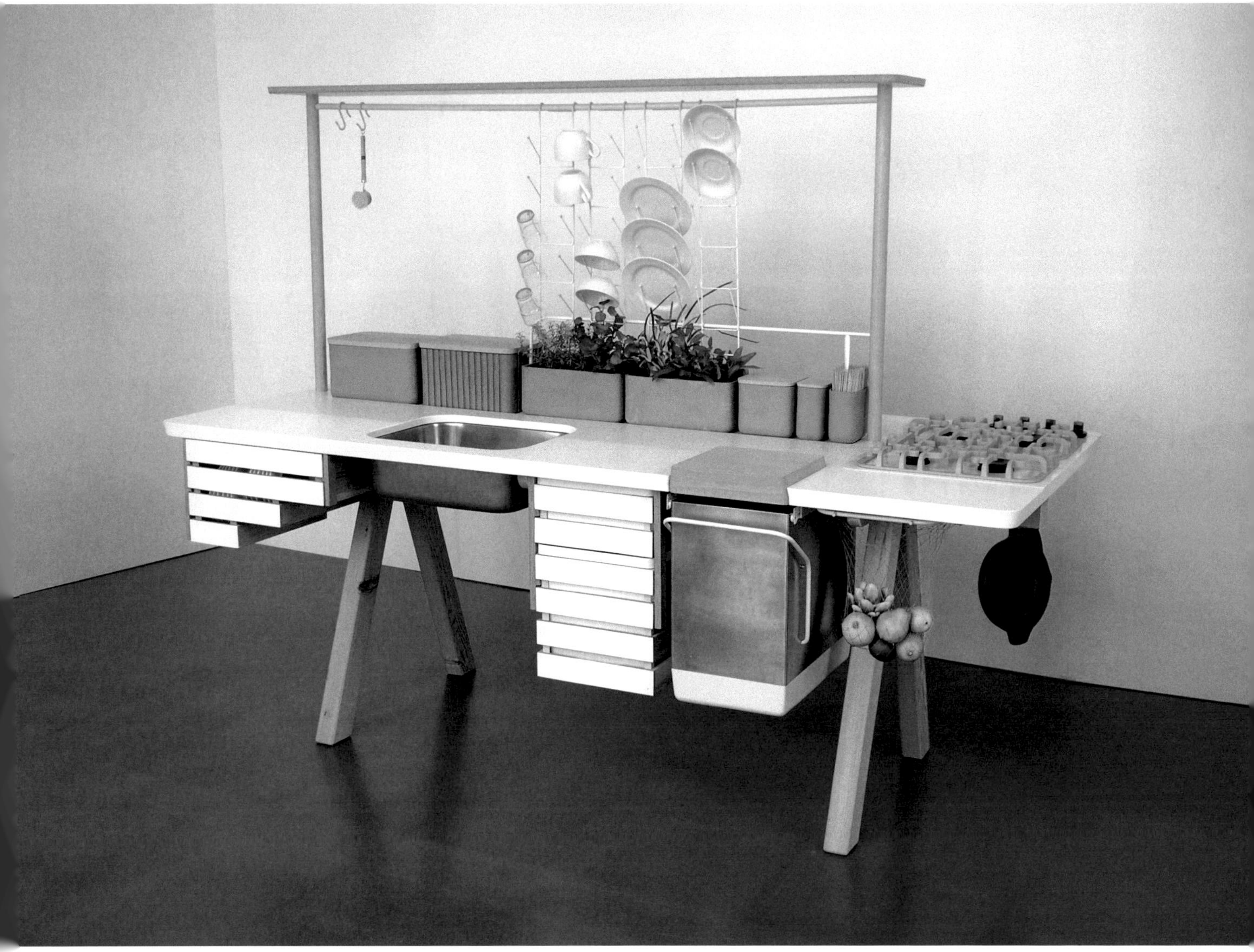

3

3, 4 Studio Gorm **Flow2**

With Flow2 Studio Gorm created a living kitchen where nature and technology are integrated in a symbiotic relationship, and processes flow into one another in a natural cycle, efficiently utilizing energy, waste, water, and other natural resources. Flow2 provides a space not only for preparing food but also an environment that gives a better understanding of how natural processes work. The Flow products can be used independently but are far more effective when they work in concert as part of a larger system. The hanging dish rack for example, offers vertical storage for drying dishes saving valuable counter space, and water from the dish rack drips onto the herbs and edible plants grown in the planter boxes below.

Photos: Studio Gorm

4

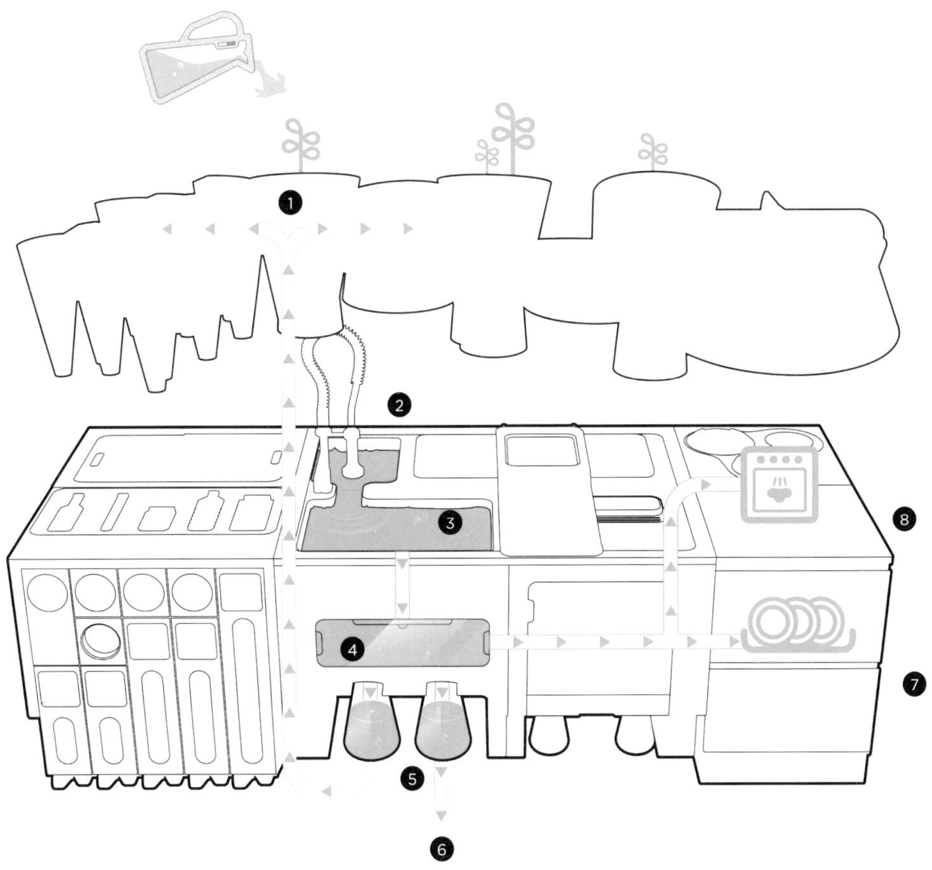

1 - Alimentation des pots ultraponiques
Watering of ultraponic pots
2 - Bac à légumes Tray for vegetables
3 - Évier Sink
4 - Réservoir Reservoir
5 - Brocs Pitchers
6 - Arrosage des plantes
Watering plants
7 - Alimentation lave-vaisselle
Input dishwasher
8 - Alimentation four vapeur
Input steam oven

FALTAZI

Ekokook

The conceptual kitchen system **Ekokook** by French designers Laurent Lebot and Victor Massip focuses on the four essentials: waste management, kitchen health, reduction and consumption of energy, and intelligent storage. In order to process waste as closely as possible to the point where it is produced, the kitchen has built-in fittings for selecting, processing, and storing organic, solid, and liquid waste. Fresh products are grown directly in the kitchen and the electrical appliances consume less energy, such as a twin-tier dishwasher, a steam oven, and a refrigerator with compartments. All materials that were used are long-lasting and have the least possible negative impact on the environment.

Philips Design
Philips Design Food Probe: Biosphere Home Farm
Biosphere Home Farm is a concept that was designed within the **Philips Design Food Probe** program and explores the possibility of growing food at home. The vertical farm contains fish, crustaceans, algae, plants, and other mini-ecosystems, all interdependent and in balance with each other.
Image: © Philips Design – Food Probes

Mathieu Lehanneure
Local River
Home storage unit for live freshwater fish combined with a mini vegetable patch.
Photo: Gaetan Robillard

Duende Studio with Mathieu Lehanneur, Benjamin Graindorge, and Eric Jourdan
Domestic Ponds
Dealing with aquaponic agriculture, **Domestic Ponds** make use of the symbiosis of fish and plants. The fish water full of nitrate-rich waste nourishes the plants, which play the role of a natural filter by retaining the nitrates and assist in maintaining balanced water for the fish.

1 Benjamin Graindorge
Liquid Garden
Mouth blown glass, sand, water-plants, water, fishes.

2 Mathieu Lehanneur
Fontaine
Aquarium, sand filter, and plant pot.

3 Eric Jourdan
Castle
Hand-turned ceramic, sand, water-plants, water, fishes.

Photos: © Ulysse Fréchelin

1

2

3

4 Juliette Warmenhoven
Potato Music Box
Photo: Juliette Warmenhoven

5, 6 Specimen Editions
Duplex
Photo: Specimen Editions - Gabriel de Vienne

4

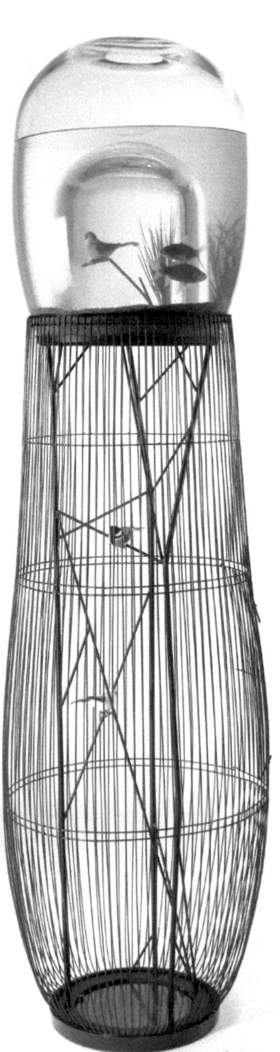

6

Bétillon / Dorval-Bory

Paysages en Exil

Paysages en Exil was a project that sought to create an experimental journey alongside La Grave hospital in Toulouse, in which the visitor was invited to explore an unlikely landscape, a condensation of climates, and a mix of nature from all over the world. In a so-called acclimatization space—a long agricultural greenhouse—medicinal plant seedlings (a reference to the hospital) from the five continents were prepared. The journey began as the visitors entered an infinite-seeming, bright tunnel and felt the climatic distortion. After blindly choosing one of the 2,000 plants that were put in white paper bags ready to be picked up, the visitor continued the journey, entering a thick cloud, a dense mist created by spraying water from the Garonne river through 1,000 nozzles on the Viguerie footbridge. At the end of this vaporous trail, a surprising garden welcomed the visitors, inviting them to plant the seedling that they had carried all the way through the misty tunnel.

Photos: Bétillon / Dorval-Bory

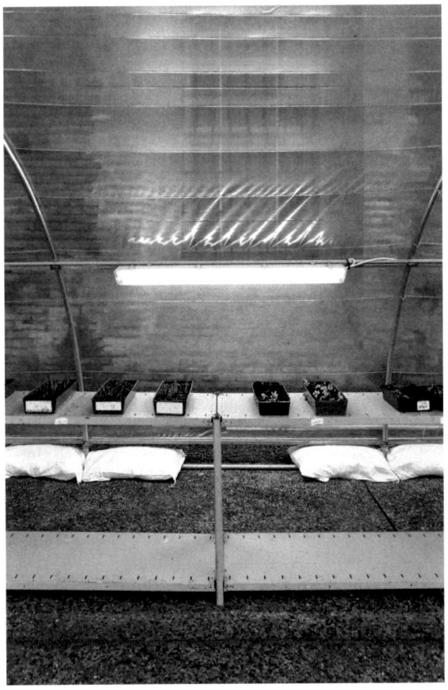

Sophia Martineck
Greenhouse

1

1 Jochem Faudet Grow Your Own Greenhouse

Small greenhouse and showcase forming a self-sufficient system, including a watering system, ventilation, temperature control, shading, allowance for different pot sizes, and space for garden tools. The greenhouse collects and stores its own rainwater and has an automatic pump for daily distribution of water.

2-4 PostCarden

Combining gift and greeting card, PostCarden is a fun and simple pop-out card that transforms into a mini living garden.

Photos: Another Studio for Design

2

3

4

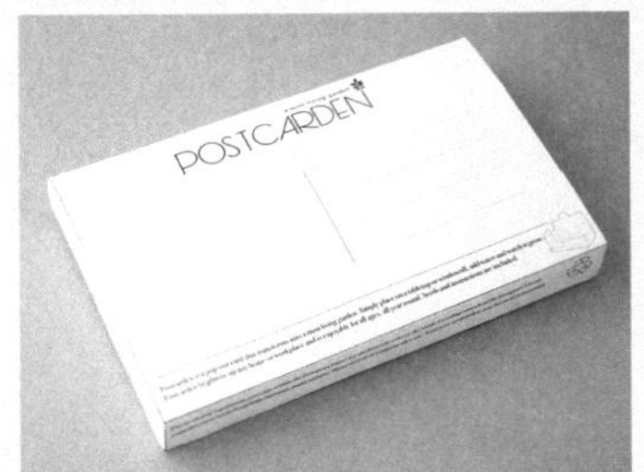

The VOLKSGARDEN™
WWW.VOLKSGARDEN.COM
US. PAT. No. 6604321
Mfg. by OMEGA GARDEN INC.
WWW.OMEGAGARDEN.COM
Made in Canada

Omega Garden

The Omega Garden is an automated carousel system, a so-called rotary garden. A rotary garden is an appliance comprised of, in this case, a 4-foot diameter cylinder that houses rows of plants growing towards a central light source. The horizontally oriented cylinder is in constant motion slowly rotating the plants 360 degrees around the central light, affording several major benefits. The Omega design provides the optimal plant-to-light-source relationship to every plant in the garden, unlike in a flat garden, where this optimal light reaches only the central plants. A cylinder yields an increased surface growing area of pi (3.14) over the footprint that the unit occupies, and this increase is multiplied by stacking the units. The rotating plants are stressed by constantly changing gravitational forces, increasing growth rates, bioflavinoids, and fiber yields; they are also self-pollinating. Without the need for direct sunlight the Omega Garden systems can be operated in insulated buildings, under increased atmospheric pressures, using a small fraction of the shrinking resources available for traditional agriculture such as land, water, fertilizer, labor, transportation, or packaging.

Photos: Ted Marchildon

Detroit Tree of Heaven Woodshop
Adaption Laboratory
Greenhouse operated on exhaust air built around an ailanthus seedling imported from Detroit. The Adaption Laboratory was installed at KW Institute for Contemporary Art, Berlin in 2004.
Photo: Ingo Vetter

opposite page **Windowfarms**

Windowfarms, invented by artist Britta Riley, are vertical, hydroponic, modular, low-energy, high-yield, edible window gardens built using low-impact or recycled local materials. Through window farming city dwellers can easily and inexpensively grow their own food in their apartment or office windows throughout the year.

Photo: Rebecca Bray, Sydney Shen, Lindsey Castillo, Britta Riley

1

1-3 Studio Makkink & Bey

The Bell Garden

The Bell Garden is a gardening concept for the "Blown to Life" exhibition in the National Glass Museum of Leerdam, referring to the technique of cloche farming. Developed in the 19th century by the French, cloche farming can be considered the ancestor of the greenhouse, where the glass protects the shoots of young plants. Together with Kenyan glass blowers, Studio Makkink & Bey blew bell-jar cloches made from used orange juice, coca cola, and beer bottles with added handles in various shapes.

Photos: Studio Makkink & Bey

3

4

4-6 100Landschaftsarchitektur Thilo Folkerts

Dachgarten Hubert Bächler

The art project Dachgarten Hubert Bächler took place on a roof terrace in Zürich in 2002. Nearby, two rivers run parallel separated merely by a wall. The project consisted of eight standard, transparent plastic bags that were filled either with water from the muddy river Sihl, water from the clear river Limmat, or with tap water. The aim of the experiment was to investigate the effects of the different types of water on the plants.

Photos: © Thilo Folkerts

5

6

FULGURO | Cédric Decroux + Yves Fidalgo

Waternetworks Drops

Collection of products centered on water consumption including a device for collecting rainwater for plants, an umbrella stand where the falling drips water a plant, and a carafe with spout for drinking water and sprinkling holes for watering plants.

Photo: FULGURO

opposite page

reHOUSE/BATH

reHOUSE/BATH is a research platform for sustainable and ethical design, focusing on the bathroom, thought of as a biotope where nature and mankind interact. The basin's evacuation system is connected to a series of plants that retain the water used for washing. Thus, the user must adapt the water consumption to the number of surrounding plants.

Photo: Geoffrey Cottenceau

1 Bas van der Veer Design
Raindrop
Rain barrel with watering can.
Photo: Astrid Zuidema

2, 3 Jochem Faudet
Freeloader
Freeloader is a site-specific growing environment utilizing existing architectural structures. Outside, rainwater is collected and stored in a tank from the drainage. Inside, by the window, plants can safely grow and are automatically watered by a gravity fed system from the tank outside.

4, 5 Innovo Design
Green Trace

6 COMMONStudio
(C)urban Ecology: Thinking Beyond the Gutter
(C)urban Ecology is a modular micro-remediation infrastructure that provides opportunities for water permeation and street vegetation, while sequestering small-scale debris before it reaches the urban watershed.
Image: Daniel Phillips

1

2

3

4

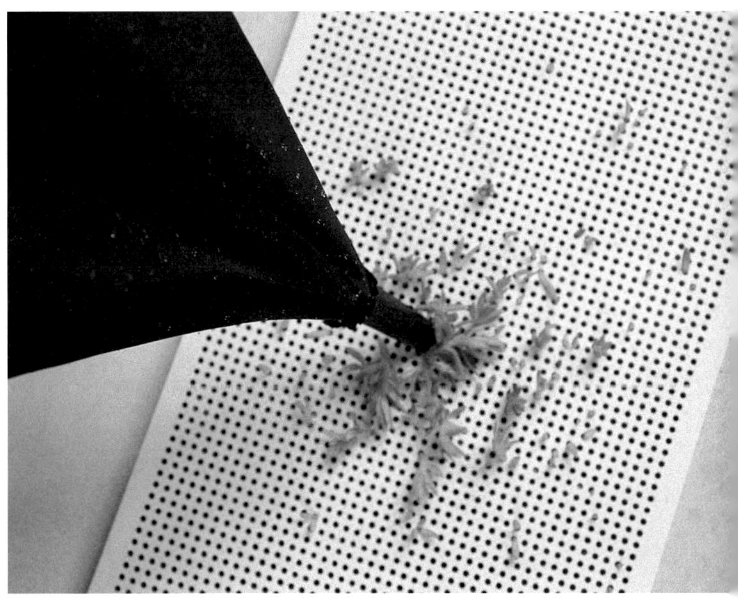
5

6

Julio Radesca
Personal Fresh Air
Photo: Julio Radesca

1 Florent Coirier/
DAILYart DESIGN
Kusamono
Horticultural lighting dedicated to the growth of plants in domestic places.
Photo: Florent Coirier

2, 3 Miriam Aust
Vase & Leuchte / Wohnbeet

1

2

3

NATURAL FUSE

NATURAL
FUSE
SHOP
ALOKA
NAZAZU
ZURE
5Kg-ko
landare

CO_2 SEQUESTERED BY PLANTS IN THE SYSTEM **OFFSETS** CO_2 RELEASED BY PRODUCTION OF ELECTRICITY CONSUMED IN THE SYSTEM

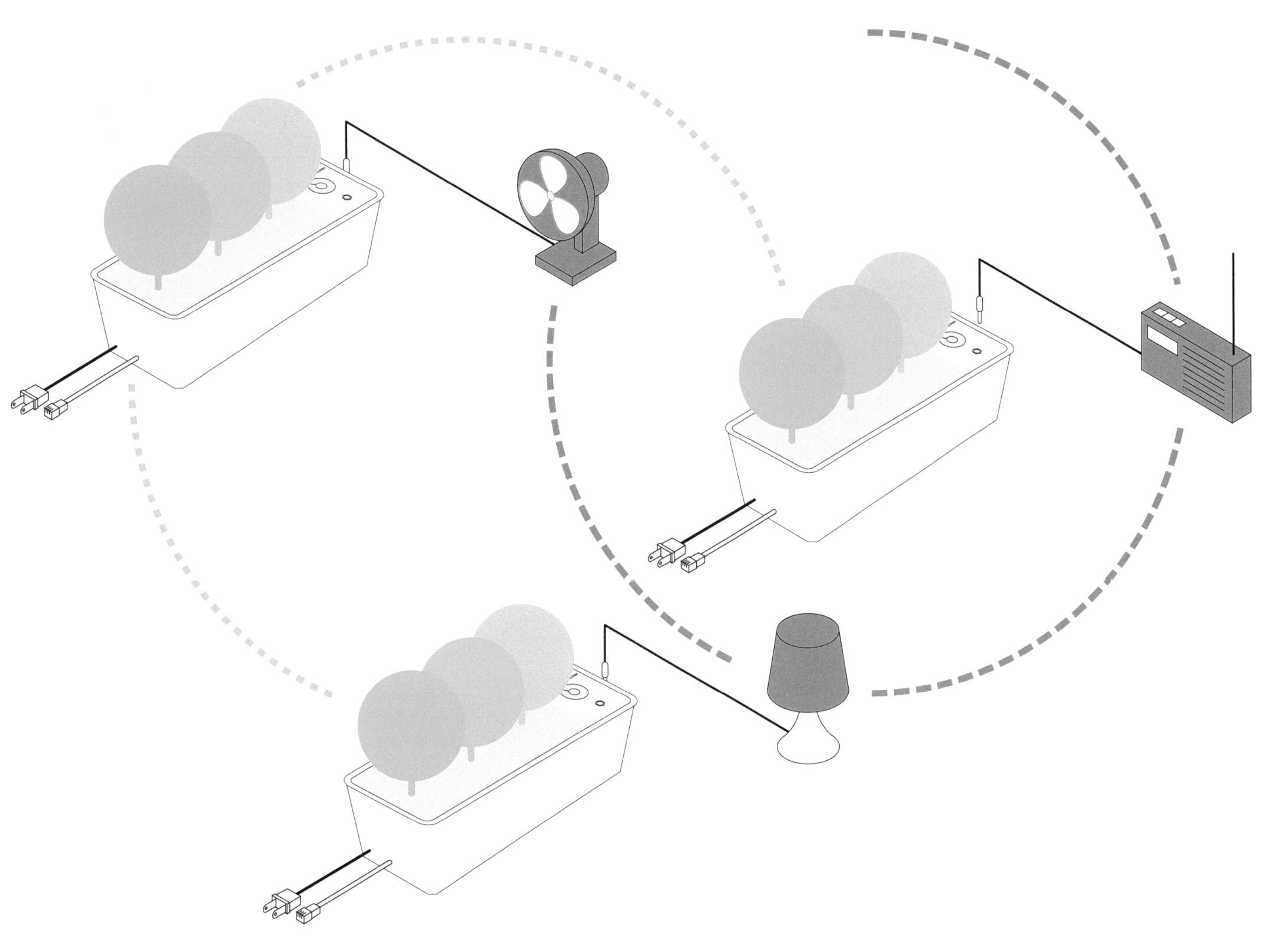

Haque Design + Research **Natural Fuse**

Natural Fuse is a micro-scale carbon dioxide overload protection framework that harnesses the carbon-sinking capabilities of plants.

Images: Haque Design + Research

1, 2 dotmancando

A.T.R.E.E.M.

The A.T.R.E.E.M. (Automated Tree-Rental for Emission Encaging Machine) project aims to criticize the carbon trading system as well as raise environmental awareness. A.T.R.E.E.M. is a renting meter attached to the tree with a tape that measures how much CO_2 is being absorbed by the tree. The user interface shows the amount and equates that to how much CO_2 we are expending.

Images: dotmancando

1

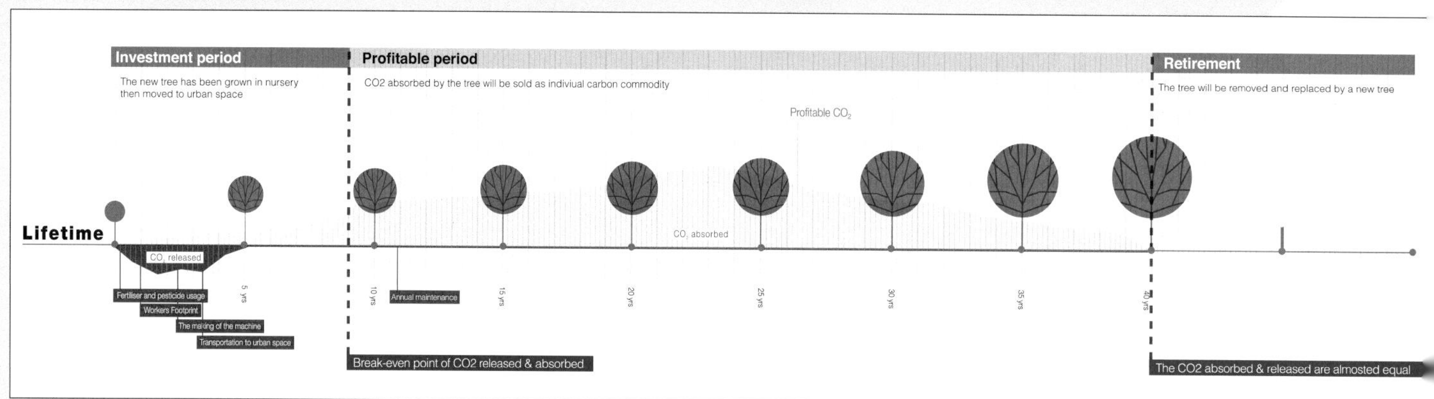

3 Botanicalls

System that allows a plant to place phone calls when it needs water.

4

5

4, 5 Inclusive Studio
Pond
Sound trumpet designed to capture the sound of the forest.
Photos: Pedro Pegenaute

Arik Levy Nature vs. Technology

Israeli-born Arik Levy is a designer, artist, technician, photographer, and filmmaker, whose works are often inspired by natural forms. Logs, rocks, and diamonds are recurring elements in his designs, as well as the theme of absence. "Life is a system of signs and symbols," he says, "where nothing is quite as it seems." In his work Nature vs. Technology the juxtaposition of genetically modified wooden logs and high frequency light technology —set up in multiple positions to resemble fire logs and flames—raises the question of what represents the contrast between the two in everyday life. Inlayed between the wooden logs, the light emitting plate illuminates micro spaces between them, symbolizing fire that is not hot but cold.

Photos: © Morgane Le Gall

Florian Rexroth
Bäume der Stadt
For his "Trees of the City" project photographer **Florian Rexroth** isolated trees from their urban context using white cloth.

P
mit Parkschein oder
Bewohnerausweis
für Zone 17
Mo–Fr 9–19h
Sa 9–14h
Welserstraße
Geisbergstraße
P

Helen Nodding
Hideaway
Miniature world inside the gap in a brick wall.
Photos: Helen Nodding

Emilio Ambasz & Associates
ACROS (Asian Crossroads Over the Sea)/Fukuoka Prefectural International Hall
Building and terraced garden in Fukuoka, Japan.

Emilio Ambasz & Associates
ACROS (Asian Crossroads Over the Sea)/Fukuoka Prefectural International Hall

Triptyque
Harmonia 57
Studio in São Paulo, Brazil.
Photos:
1, 2 Nelson Kon;
3 Leonardo Finotti

2

3

Mass Studies
Ann Demeulemeester Shop
Seoul, Korea
Photos: Yong-Kwan Kim

Patrick Blanc
Mur Végétal

French botanist **Patrick Blanc** has been planting vertical gardens long before the term became a household name. In 1988, he patented his idea of the **Mur Végétal**, for which he installs PVC panels on walls and facades, covers them with non-biodegradable felt and cuts pockets for the plants to slot in. Over time, a soil-less botanical mural appears, that can cover anything from a small wall to whole buildings, encased in greenery. The system is based on the principle of stratification, which one finds in tropical climates, offering the flora an almost unlimited shelf-life, provided they are regularly fertilized and watered with the help of a simple watering system. The advantage of such vertical wall gardens over horizontal ones is that they need less space. They only use up unutilized areas; they don't steal any space in densely populated areas. Through the choice of plant and the vertical bias, the plants spread themselves steeply downward instead of, as on the ground, upward and sideways at the same time. Thus, twice as much can be planted. By now **Patrick Blanc** has installed 161 of his vertical gardens all around the world.

1 CaixaForum, Madrid

2 Musee Du Quai Branly, Paris

Photos: Patrick Blanc

1

2

cheungvogl
Shinjuku Gardens
Parking garage in Tokyo, Japan.
Images: cheungvogl

2

Bureau Baubotanik
1, 3 Plattform in der Steveraue
The bearing structure of the platform consists of living trees that have fused together. Due to their diameter growth, conventional, technical components grow into the plant. Thus, a supporting structure is interlockingly formed over the growth process of the tree and makes it possible to construct gardens and parks vertically. Photos:
Photos:
1 Britta Biermann;
3 Bureau Baubotanik

2 Der Steg
Photo: Storz, Schwertfeger, Ludwig;

3

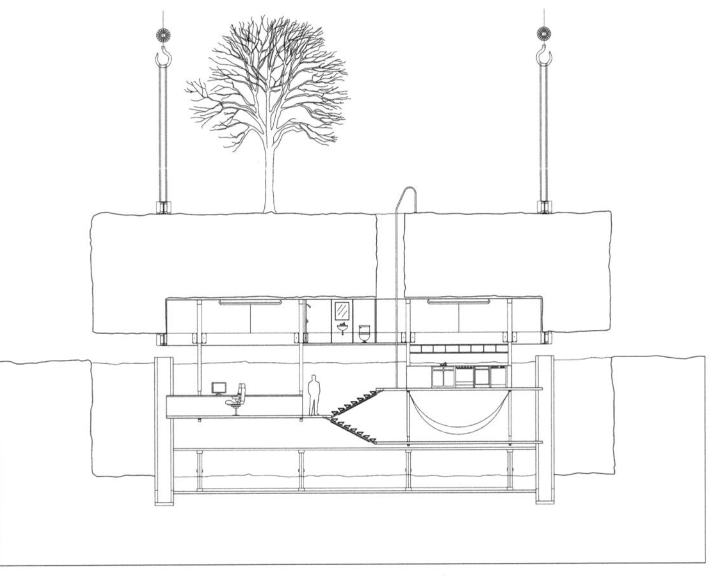

Marcelo Ertorteguy
The Stone
The Stone is a concept design of a hovering house: a petrified piece of soil cut and lifted into the air, acting as an inhabitable cloud.

FARMING IN THE FUTURE

As the world population continuously grows, humanity is faced with the challenge of growing more and more food. It is estimated that by the year 2050, the human population will have increased by about three billion people. The amount of land needed in order to grow enough crops to feed them equates to about 20 % more land than is represented by the country of Brazil. While working with students, microbiologist and professor of environmental health at Columbia University Dickson Despommier developed the idea of vertically growing plants indoors. Ever since he introduced the first outline of his idea to the public in 2001, scientists and architects have been working on various concepts seeking to realize farmscrapers equipped with greenhouse technology that allow year-round production of fruit, vegetables, and algae in cities.

Arup
Vertical Farm Concept Sketch
General concept for a generic dense urban context.

1

2

3

4

WORK Architecture Company

1 Locavore Fantasia

WORK Architecture Company's version of vertical farming combines migrant farmers' housing in a series of stepped terraces with a farmer's market and public space below. The terraces allow in-soil growing and a small golf course, duplicating the surface of the site. The entire project is supported, literally, by culture with sculpture-structures holding it up. The **Locavore Fantasia** project was commissioned by New York magazine.

2-4 Plug Out

Invited to propose a vision for the future of Manhattan's Greenwich South neighborhood, **WORK Architecture Company** was assigned a site whose access to sunlight was blocked by a large building immediately to the south. Noticing that no one was using the airspace over West Street–an enormous 10-lane boulevard–the architecture firm proposed a series of experimental new housing typologies, stacked in a 45-story building and expressed as independent sections, rotated around the building's core and out above West Street. This Swiss Army Knife approach takes full advantage of sunlight and views and allows each section's rooftop to become a different ecosystem, from urban farms to campgrounds to streams and rivers. The idea behind the concept is that the building can also provide the necessary ecological infrastructure for the Greenwich South neighborhood, allowing it to plug out from the city grid and perform a kind of urban dialysis: filtering and cleaning water and providing energy, which is then fed back into the surrounding district. The tower's core, linking the various sections with structure and vertical transportation, also contains this entire infrastructure. Rainwater is harvested for toilets, irrigation, hydroponic farming, laundry, and fish farming. Gray-water is cleaned in a gray-water wetland and reused in toilets and irrigation. Black water is cleaned and recycled in a treatment facility and moved back up the tower to be used for cooling the energy systems. Heat and energy are created in several ways: via composting, a "waste to power incinerator," geothermal heating, solar powered facades, traffic wind turbines, and a co-generation plant. Excess heat is used to create public baths, a hot yoga center, and warmed earth for the urban campgrounds, allowing year-round use.

Images:
3 Elizabeth Felicella;
all others WORK Architecture Company

1

2

3

4

Tjep.
1 Oogst 1
Concept for a one-bedroom house that provides its resident with food, energy, heat, and oxygen.

2–4 Oogst 1000
Oogst 1000 Wonderland is a concept for a self-sufficient farm, restaurant, hotel, and amusement park for 1000 people. All food for the restaurant comes from the central structure and directly adjacent fields. Hotel guests are also the farmers, staying for free when working. Original Dutch farm buildings have been implemented but the traditional layout of the farm has been completely re-arranged. The technology is based on a greenhouse-powered, self-sustainable system. The entire process is visible to the visitor, giving the complex a didactic function as to new agricultural developments. **Oogst 1000 Wonderland** toilets are also linked to a biogas energy system, so **Oogst 1000** offers the world's first toilets where people actually get paid 50 cents per visit.

5, 6 Amsterdam City Garden
Concept for greenhouses in Amsterdam, Netherlands.

Images: Tjep.

5

6

AGENCY

Super Levee Urban Farm

Super Levee Urban Farm proposes a global system of levees, serving also as a new brand of urban farms at the city's edge, preserving local ecologies while protecting cities from the dangers of rising sea levels and water-borne disasters.

Images: © 2010 by AGENCY Architecture LLC

1

1 UP Projects
Spontaneous City in the Tree of Heaven
Photo: London Fieldworks, courtesy of UP Projects

2 Luís Porém
APA – Abrigo Para Aves

3 Studiomama
Bird Frame
Photo: Richard Davis

2

3

1

1-4 Kieren Jones The Chicken Project

With his Chicken Project artist Kieren Jones explored an eco-sustainable way of utilizing all the parts of a single chicken. Jones made china pieces from ground bones, tanned chicken leather from which he made a flight jacket with feather downing, and turned bones into salt spoons and wishbones.

Photos: Kieren Jones

5

5 Frederick Roijé
Breed Retreat
Photo: Dylan van Keulen

2

3

4

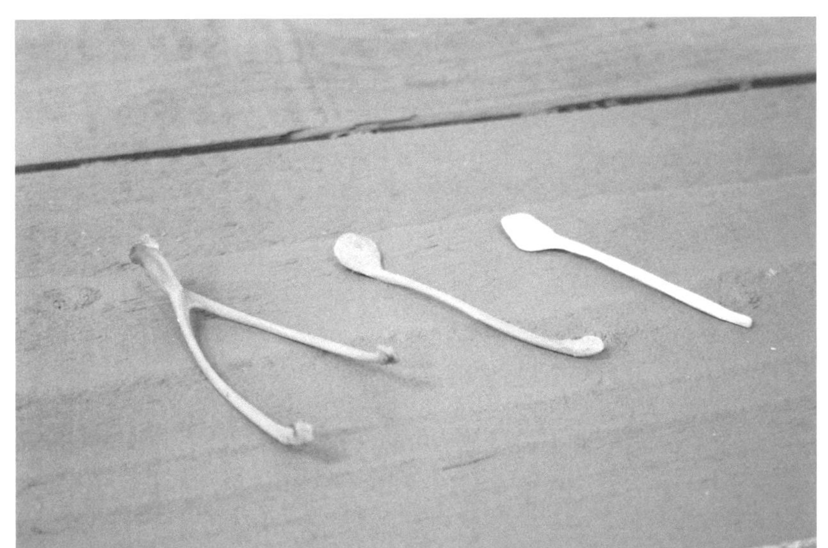

1

1 Arup
Insect Hotel – Beyond the Hive
2010
Photo: James Ward

2 Ants of the Prairie
Bat Tower
Bat house prototype, exploring strategies for increasing public awareness of bats as a critical component of the ecosystem.
Photo: Albert Chao

2

3, 4 Tuur Van Balen Pigeon d'Or

Developed by Belgian designer Tuur Van Baalen, Pigeon d'Or proposes the use of feral pigeons as a platform and interface for synthetic biology in an urban environment by attempting to make a pigeon defecate soap. Through modification of the animal's metabolism—specifically the bacteria that live in their gut—synthetic biology might add new functionality to animals that are commonly condemned as being flying rats. The pigeons would be fed specially designed bacteria that turns feces into detergent and is as harmless to pigeons as yoghurt is to humans. Through the pursuit of manipulating pigeon excrement and designing appropriate architectural interfaces, the project explores the ethical, political, practical, and aesthetic consequences of designing biology.

Photos: In collaboration with James Chappell

3

Arik Levy Giant Rock

Giant Rock is part of a series entitled "Bigger than Man" where Arik Levy experienced the object we are looking at becoming a counterbalance in space, a new gravity of both visual and emotional parameters. At first sight, the Giant Rock appears to be simply what it is: a big rock. At second glance the beholder realizes that the meteorite is juxtaposing man and nature. It is about what is not there, the absence, it is the pieces that are taken out that make it exist. Built of a non-geological growth, Giant Rock is both hard and soft, micro-macro, a mere light reflection as well as an optical and emotional experience. The rock, in true stealth fashion, disappears and reappears by reflecting the beholder and his environment. The sculpture was created in 2009 and is a permanent installation in a private collection in France.

Photo: © Arik Levy

Nils Holger Moormann
Walden
Fully equipped garden shed.
Photos: © Jäger & Jäger

1

1 24H Architecture
Dragspelhuset at Övre Gla
Photo: Boris Zeisser

2 Studio Weave
Freya's Cabin
Photo: Peter Sharpe

3 ryan lingard design
Signal Shed
Photo: Ryan Lingard

4 Rogier Martens
Build-It-Yourself Treehouse
(De Zelfbouwboomhut)
Photo: AANDEBOOM

5 Olgga Architectes
Flake House
Photo: Fabienne Delafraye

3

4

2

ZENDOME.ecopod

Ecopod

The Ecopod Boutique Retreat is nestled amongst birch trees and rhododendrons at Loch Linnhe in Scotland. The pods sit on a wooden decking platform and feature 70 square meters of light-filled space. Inside, the modern open-plan design and classic furniture are combined with quirky traditional touches of stags' antlers and natural sheepskins.

Photos: Jim Milligan

3

1 Garrett Finney
Cricket Trailer
Photo: David Bates

2, 3 import.export
Architecture
Urban Camping
Concept for an urban camping tower.
Photos: import.export
Architecture

The Grand Daddy
Airstream Penthouse
Trailer Park
Trailer park on the roof of the **Grand Daddy** hotel in Cape Town, South Africa.

Kevin van Braak

Caravan 02

When opened, the Caravan 02 manifests itself as an artificial park featuring stuffed animals, artificial grass, silk flowers and trees, a sound installation with bird sounds, and a BBQ.

Pushak Moss Your City

Norwegian architectural practice Pushak has designed an installation for The Architecture Foundation featuring a spectacular undulating moss landscape. The brief was to design an active hub within the festival for people to gather and debate, exploring the relationship between contemporary architecture and Norway's landscape and natural resources, while also responding to local conditions in London. Moss Your City was inspired by the Norwegian landscape and refers to the Bankside Urban Forest, which aims to enhance public spaces —including streets, pavements, squares, and parks—in the Bankside area. For Moss Your City Pushak used the idea of green guerilla actions like moss graffiti and the general idea of greening bleak surfaces of the city to informally advertise the forest concept and give it a stronger presence in people's minds.

Photo: Guy Archard

3

1, 2 Makoto Azuma
Time of Moss
Grown on the biodegradable fiber Terramac, shown at Milan Design Week 2009.
Photos: Shiinoki Shunsuke

3 i29
Home 06
Private residence in Amsterdam.
Photo: i29 | interior architects

4 Patrick Blanc
Centre Commercial,
Les Passages,
Boulogne-Billancourt
Photo: Patrick Blanc

4

1-3 Studio Job
Bavaria
Bavaria Bench and **Bavaria Mirror** are pieces from a furniture collection made from Indian rosewood and decorated with farm imagery using laser-cut inlays.
Photos: R. Kot

4 Meritalia
Montanara
Sofa designed by Gaetano Pesce.
Photo: Meritalia Spa

1

2

4

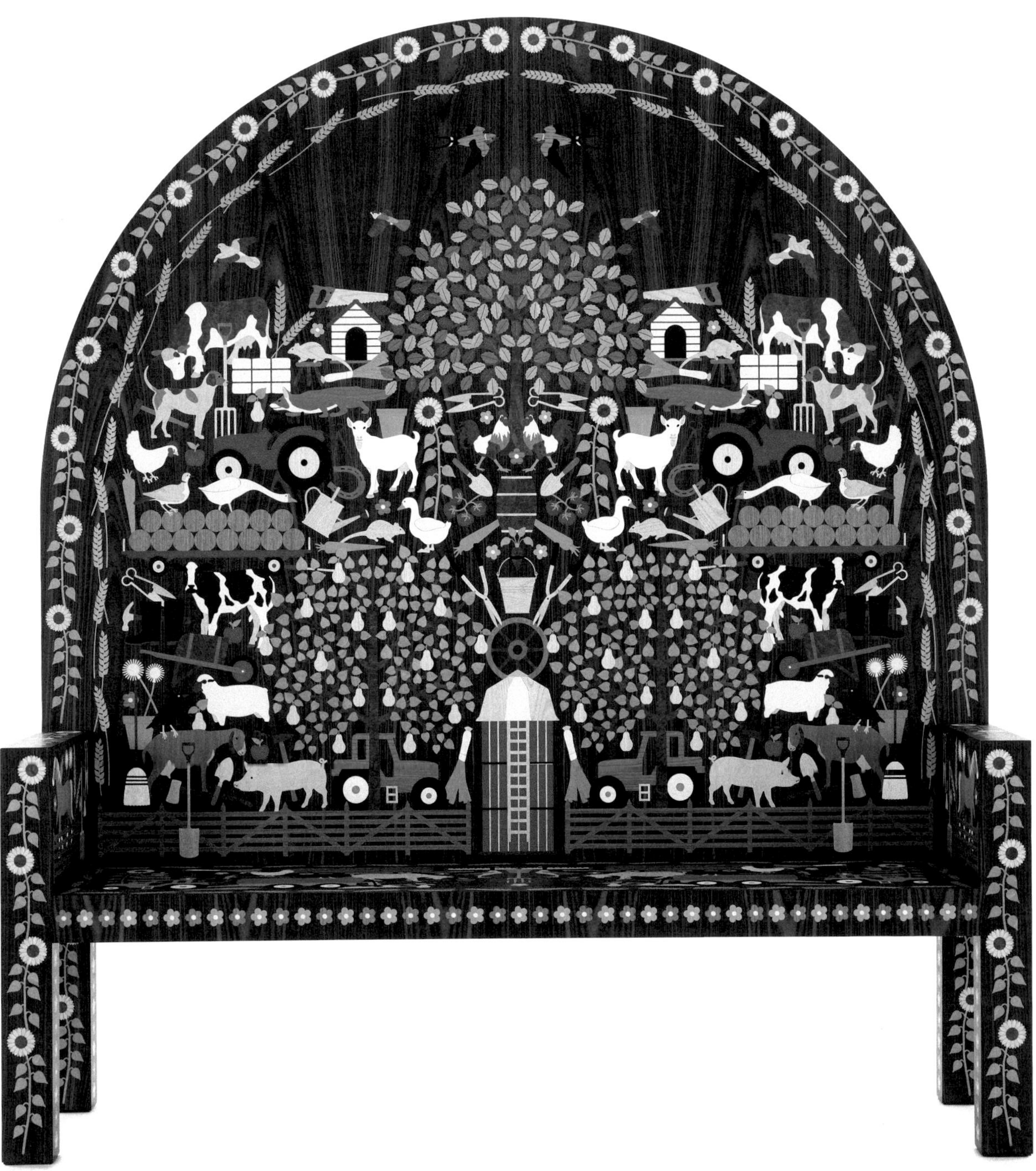

3

Heatherwick Studio

UK Pavilion at the 2010 Shanghai Expo

For the design of the UK Pavilion Heatherwick Studio sought an approach that would engage meaningfully with Shanghai Expo's theme, "Better City, Better Life" and stand out from the anticipated trend for technology driven pavilions, filled with audio-visual content on screens, projections, and speakers. In collaboration with a wider project team, the studio developed the idea of the UK Pavilion exploring the relationship between nature and cities. Rather than creating a conventional advertisement for the UK, this was a subject that could make a real contribution to the Expo's theme; London is the greenest city of its size in the world, the UK pioneered the world's first ever public park and the world's most renowned botanical institution, the Royal Botanic Gardens, Kew. Heatherwick Studio came up with the idea of involving Kew's Millennium Seed Bank partnership whose mission is to collect the seeds of 25 % of the world's plant species by 2020. The design process evolved to produce two interlinked and experiential elements: an architecturally iconic Seed Cathedral, and a multi-layered landscape treatment of the 6,000-square-meter site. The Seed Cathedral sits in the centre of the UK Pavilion's site, 20 meters in height, formed from 60,000 slender transparent fiber optic rods, each 7.5 meters long and each encasing one or more seeds at its tip. During the day, they draw daylight inwards to illuminate the interior. At night, light sources inside each rod allow the whole structure to glow. As the wind moves past, the building and its optic "hairs" gently move to create a dynamic effect. The Seed Cathedral has been nick-named "Pu Gong Ying," meaning "The Dandelion," by the Chinese public. After the Expo, just as dandelion seeds are blown away and disperse on the breeze, the Seed Cathedral's 60,000 optic hairs, each one containing the huge potential of life, were distributed across China and the UK to hundreds of schools as a special legacy of the UK Pavilion at the 2010 Shanghai Expo.

Photos: Iwan Baan

Casagrande Laboratory

Ruin Academy

Ruin Academy in Taipei is an independent crossover architectural research center conceived by Finland-based Casagrande Laboratory and the Taiwanese JUT Foundation for Arts & Architecture. It organizes workshops and courses for various Taiwanese and international universities including the National Taiwan University Department of Sociology, Tamkang University Department of Architecture, Aalto University Sustainable Global Technologies Center, and Helsinki University of Arts and Design Department of Environmental Art. The research and design tasks oscillate between architecture, urban design, environmental art, and other disciplines of art and science within the general framework of built human environments. The Ruin Academy occupies an abandoned 5-story apartment building in central Taipei. All the interior walls of the building and all the windows have been removed in order to grow bamboo and vegetables inside the house. The whole building is penetrated with 6-inch holes in order to let rain inside. Professors and students sleep and work in dormitories made from mahogany and have a public sauna on the fifth floor at their disposal.

Photos: AdDa

Casagrande Laboratory
Ruin Academy
Photos: AdDa

Adi Zaffran Weisler
RAWtation
Collection of tables and chairs combining rotationally molded plastic and wood.
Photo: Oded Antman

Naomi Reis
Florescent (Out of the Ruins)
Art installation.

opposite page
Weeds
Painting from the series Vertical Gardens, which features mutated modernist skyscrapers festooned with plant life.
Photo: Etienne Frossard Photography

1

2

1, 2 Nick Bastis
Nature Always Wins/
Vegetated Wall
Photo: Giacomo Fortunato

3 Pour les Alpes
Crystal "Chapütschin"
Wooden planter inspired by mountain crystal.
Photo: Pour les Alpes

4 Joe Paine
Kreep Planter
Inspired by creepers, the **Kreep Planter** can be extended, changed in shape, and adapted to the wall it is mounted to. The smaller pots are intended for growing cuttings, which can be transplanted to the larger pots when big enough.

MATTEO CIBIC STUDIO
5 #03
Terrarium.
6 Domsai
Terrariums.
Photo: Lorenzo Vitturi

3

4

5

6

1

1 woollypocket
Flexible, breathable, and modular gardening containers made of 100 % recycled plastic bottles that have been industrially felted.
Photo: Jason Eric Hardwick

2 FULGURO | Yves Fidalgo + Cédric Decroux
Green Shutter
Hanging garden that regains its function as a shutter when the plants grow upwards.
Photo: Emilie Müller and Yann Gross

3 BACSAC
Light, portable planter bags made from a 100 % recyclable double-walled geotextile fabric that maintains the necessary balance between air, soil, and water.

4, 5 Greenmeme
Live Within Skin
Photos: Freya Bardell

2

3

5

4

Furnibloom
Regards from Iceland
Photos: MBL/Frikki

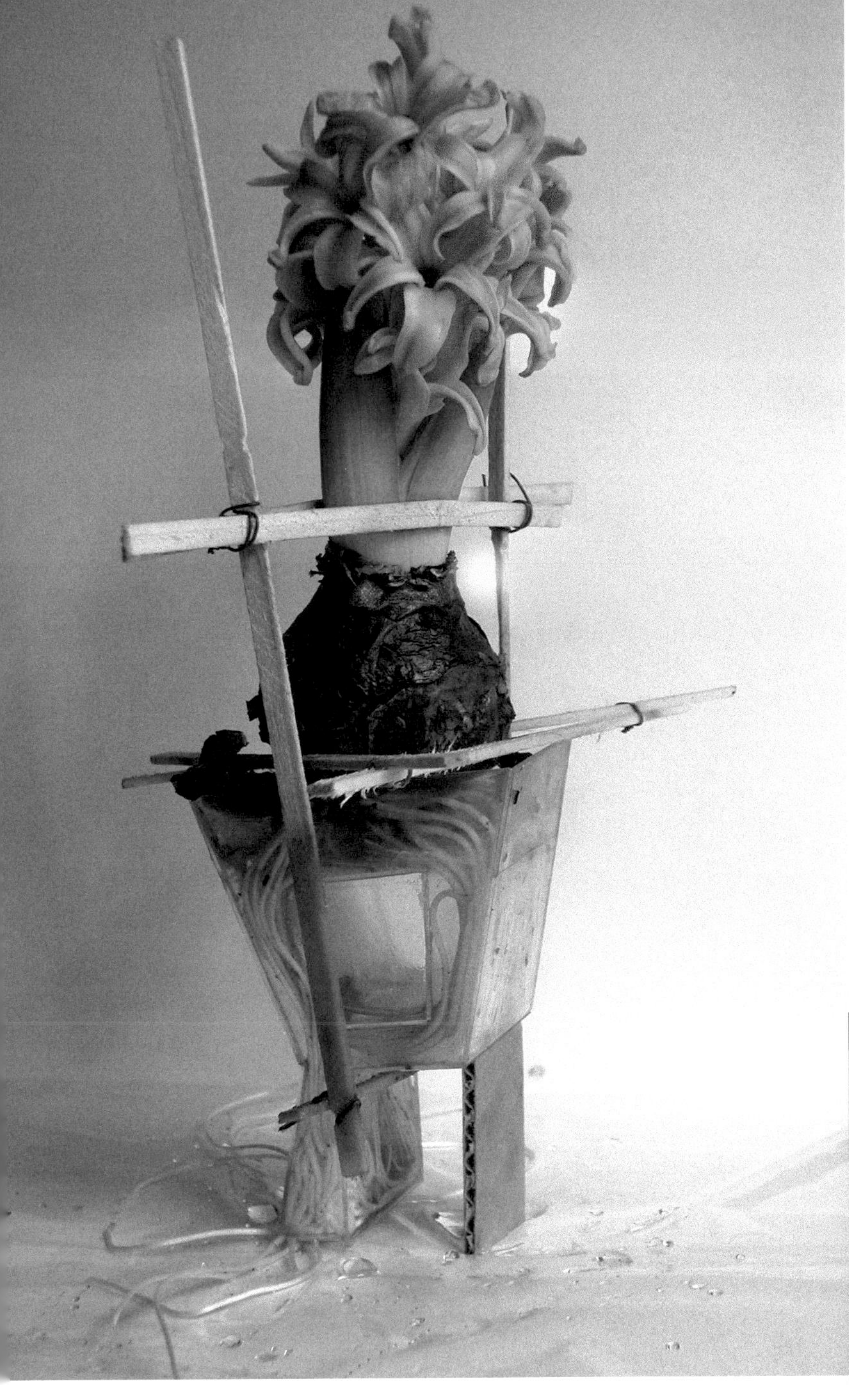

Kai Linke
Roots
Series of art works dealing with human intervention into the growth of plants.
Photos: Kai Linke

1

2

3

4

5

Studio Makkink & Bey
1, 2 Gardening Bench
Temporary outdoor seat made from compacted garden mulch, which will eventually decay into soil.
Photo: Marsel Loermans

3 Tree Trunk Bench
Photo: Marsel Loermans

4, 5 Sandbench Bulldozer
Photos: Studio Makkink & Bey assisted by Eric Klarenbeek

1

1 Paul Loebach
Great Camp Collection
Paul Loebach's Great Camp Collection derives its inspiration from the Adirondack vacation culture of upstate New York in the late 1800s. The rustic look is achieved by using proprietary computerized machining techniques developed specifically for this project, capable of producing uncommonly meticulous faceted forms. This technology digitally sculpts solid wood into components reminiscent of raw sticks and branches. The parts come together using traditional joinery to make a dresser, credenza, chair, and coat stand of the finest quality and finish.
Photo: Jeremy Frechette

2 Owl Project
Log1k
Constructed from a full circle log section, the **Log1k** is a battery-operated sequencer & sampler featuring signal generators, multiple microphone inputs and eight audio outputs. A 240V fluorescent tube provides a screen-like glowing panel which also provides electrical interference. Artist group **Owl Project** designed and constructed **Log1k** to perform their own brand of electronica, which combines electro-magnetic fields and signals to produce complex beats and ambient sound.
Photo: Harriet Hall

2

Steven Burke
Poor Little Trees

THE PASSION OF OUR

Shinji Turner-Yamamoto **Global Tree Project: Hanging Garden**

For Hanging Garden, Turner-Yamamoto envisioned a live tree supported by a large inverted dead tree. The intertwined root systems of the uprooted trees created a suspended garden oriented as a tower or cross at the center of the church it was exhibited in.

Photo: Shinji Turner-Yamamoto

Mikala Dwyer
Hanging Smoking Garden
Photos: Jens Ziehe, courtesy of Hamish Morrison Galerie,
© VG Bild-Kunst, Bonn 2010

Makoto Azuma
Botanical Sculpture #1
Assemblage
Tokyo, 2008
Photos: Shiinoki Shunsuke

Janina Loeve
Divers, Bouquets to Eat Alive
Photos: © Studio Janina Loeve

Nicole Dextras
Camellia Countessa
The Weedrobes series by artist **Nicole Dextras** is mostly fabricated with edible plants that were chosen for their resemblance to ruffled and pleated fabrics. The **Camellia Countessa** dress reflects the pannier dresses of the baroque period. Pannier means basket in French and the structure for these types of dresses were originally made of willow. **Dextras** used willow branches to recreate the organic origins of this fashion.
Photo: Nicole Dextras

Makoto Azuma
Fashion in Nature
Photo: Shiinoki Shunsuke

1

2

3

4

Makoto Azuma
1 I♥湯
Naoshima, Kagawa, Japan, 2009

2 Bridge of Plants
Ark Hills, Tokyo, 2009

3 Shiki2
NRW Forum, Dusseldorf, Germany, 2008

4 Shiki1
Fukuoka, Japan, 2009

Photos: Shiinoki Shunsuke

1

2

3

Andre Woodward

1 Psychocandy

Sculpture consisting of audio equipment, stripped MP3 players, amplifiers, speakers, bonsai trees, water pumps, timers, grow lights, and steel.

2 Dual Arboretum

Sculptures consisting of asphalt excavated from potholes and fractured streets all over Southern California. The asphalt is used as sculptural enclosures for audio electronics and bonsai trees. The audio emitting from the pieces are recordings taken at the sites from which the asphalt originated.

3 Never Understand Me/ It's So Hard

For this work ficus and juniper trees were planted in soil before they were encased in cubes of concrete, which allows them to continue to grow and to eventually crack the concrete.

Photos: Andre Woodward

1

3

Brenna Murphy
Sculptural installations that model mental representations of the structure of time and space.

1 Timer

2 TimeTable

3 Food4Thought

4 GroundWork

2

4

Heidi Norton
Channeling
(Baby Spider Plants)

opposite page Frank Bruggeman
1 Catalpa (Solitaire
Is the Only Game in Town)
Forests, maize fields, open pastures, and a huge solitary oak: that is Northern Brabant's landscape in a nutshell. Artist **Frank Bruggeman** puts an exotic catalpa tree right in the heart of this landscape. The catalpa is originally from East Asia and is nowadays very popular in Dutch gardens, though usually cultivated and bulb-shaped. Bruggeman's specimen will grow in its natural shape.

2 Natureobject #1
Installation combining native and exotic plants.
Photo: collection of Museum Boijmans Van Beuningen, Rotterdam

3 Local Botanica
Installation in cooperation with VU Hortus Amsterdam researching the diversity of species in regional nature.

2

3

1

2

1, 2 Frank Bruggeman
Flux Flying Flower Show
Installation with 15 flower pieces in the setting of a photo studio. Visitors of the Flux/S festival had the opportunity to get their photo taken next to a bouquet of late-summer flowers.

3 Ernst van der Hoeven
Flux Flying Flower Show, Pumpkin Arena
Photo: Ernst van der Hoeven

3

1

Byggstudio Vintage Plant Shop

In May 2008 Markus Bergström and Simon Jones opened a temporary Vintage Plant Shop in the Hornstull area of Stockholm. The shop worked as a plant market where people could donate, exchange, or buy a Vintage Plant. A Vintage Plant Archive was displayed, consisting of the plants' background stories and photos. Ceramicists Linus Ersson and Andrea Djerf were invited to make flower-pots. During the summer about 150 plants were donated to the project and given new homes.

Photos:
1 Simon Jones;
all others Byggstudio

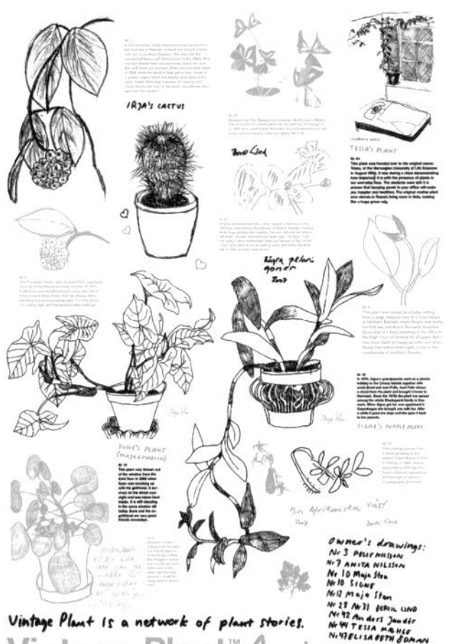

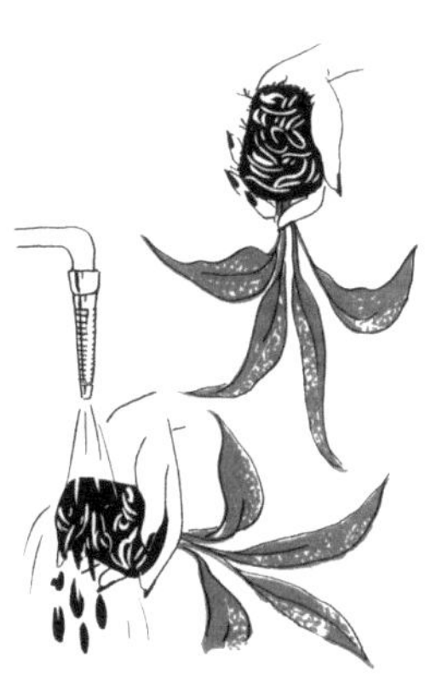

breadedEscalope design studio

Grow to Go

Austrian design studio breadedEscalope has given a new identity to Vienna flower shop Wildwuchs, mimicking the concept of fast food companies, including the packaging. Various seeds and soil mixes are sold in burger boxes and paper cups.

Photo: breadedEscalope design studio

Scheltens & Abbenes Studio
Bouquet IX
2008, 100 cm × 120 cm, color print mounted between dibond and perspex.

1

1 Baker Creek Heirloom Seeds
Seed Packets
Photo: Jere Gettle

2 Matchstick Garden
The tip of each match contains seeds already mixed to grow and only needs to be stuck into soil.

3 COMMONStudio
Greenaid – Seedbomb Vending
The **Greenaid** dispensary makes guerilla gardening efforts more accessible to all by appropriating the existing distribution system of the coin-operated candy machine. To date, **COMMONStudio** has placed 25 such machines across the USA in communities underserved by public green space. **Greenaid** is equally an interactive public awareness campaign, a lucrative fund-raising tool, and a beacon for small scale grass roots action that engages directly yet casually with local residents to both reveal and remedy issues of spatial inequity in their community.
Photo: Daniel Phillips

2

the commonstudio presents a GREENAID initiative
SEEDBOMBS
COMBAT THE FORGOTTEN GREY SPACES YOU ENCOUNTER EVERYDAY
GREENAID thecommonstudio.com
50¢
SEEDBOMBS
FIVE SPOT (NEMOPHILA MACULATE)
GOLDEN LUPINE (LUPINUS DENSIFLORUS)
TIDY TIPS (LAYIA PLATYGLOSSA)
MONKEYFLOWER (MIMULUS AURANTIACUS PUNICEUS)
WHITE YARROW (ACHILLEA MILLEFOLIUM)
GLOBE GILIA (GILIA CAPITATA)
MISSION RED
CALIFORNIA WILDFLOWER MIX
SEEDBOMBS

SEED BOMBS

Although seed bombs have become increasingly popular within the last couple of years, the records of aerial plantation date back to 1930, when planes were used to distribute seeds over inaccessible mountains in Hawaii after forest fires. Made from a mixture of clay soil, compost, seeds, and water to bind, seed bombs these days are the munitions of guerrilla gardeners in the fight against the neglect of public spaces. To reclaim and transform especially hard-to-reach places, seed bombs are anonymously thrown into derelict urban sites in order to transform them into places worth looking at and caring for.

3

4

1-3 Kabloom
Seedbom
Photos: Susan Castillo

4 THE END.
Guerilla Gärtner
Photo: © Alva Unger

5 Tony Minh Nguyen
Flower Grenade
Photo: Snowhome

6 Marti Guixé
Plant-me Pets
Character made from natural latex with vegetable plant seeds for eyes.
Photo: Imagekontainer/Knölke

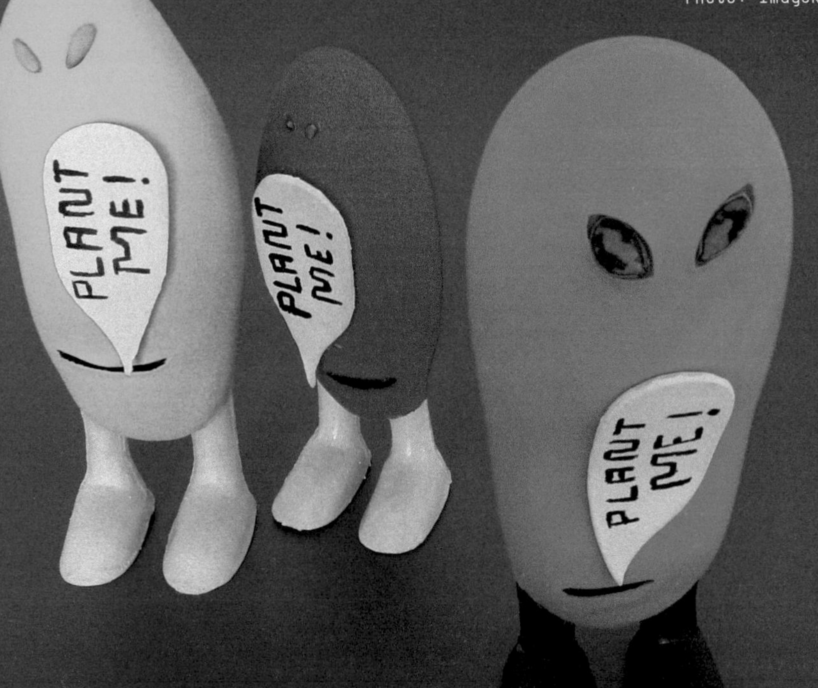

5

6

1

5

6

2

3

4

1-4 2-Round Tactical Gravity Planter & Mk II Agent Deployed Field Auger
The 2-Round Tactical Gravity Planter handbag has been created as one of a series of two objects. It accompanies the MK II Agent Deployed Field Auger, dropping plants in the holes created by the briefcase. The leather handbag contains a conveyor belt driven by a motor. When the user presses the button on the outside of the bag, the belt is activated and a plant (contained in a biodegradable pot) drops from the bottom.

5, 6 Precision Bombing Device I
The camera is intended for sowing seeds at long distances and over barriers (such as a fence). Although it appears to be a genuine camera, this piece has been fabricated from scratch. Inside, it contains a mechanism that projects small seed bullets 10-15 meters in distance.

Vanessa Harden

The Subversive Gardener

Designer Vanessa Harden has made herself a name as the "Q" of the guerrilla gardening world. Similar to the inventive James Bond character, Harden has come up with a series of nifty gadgets for activists within this growing subculture. Guerrilla gardeners secretly meet at night to illegally plant flowers, shrubs, and vegetables in neglected urban spaces. Although their actions seem harmless, they are still viewed by the authorities as illegal and prosecutable. For her Subversive Gardener project, Vanessa Harden sought various methods of disguising gardening paraphernalia in everyday attire and accessories, drawing on influences from militaria and spy gadgetry. Thus, her designs allow the guerrilla gardener to integrate their assaults into their everyday routine.

Photos: Roel Paredaens

1, 2 Guerrilla Gardening

Lavender Traffic Island

Lavender pillows filled with herbs harvested from Lavender Traffic Island.

Photos: Richard Reynolds

2

1

3 Filthy Luker
Paranoid Bush
Photo: Filthy Luker

4 Sandrine Estrade Boulet
Pom-Pom Girl
Photo: Sandrine Estrade Boulet

3

4

1

ROA
1 Squirrel Williamsburg
Photo: by the artist

2 No title
Photo: by the artist

3 Lenticular Rabbit
Photo: RomanyGW

2

3

Sebastian Errazuris **The Day Cows Fly**

Cow rescued from its death in a slaughter-house and taken to a recreated farm on the top of a 10-story building in the center of Santiago, Chile.

1

2

Buero fuer Gestaltung

Kuhwatching Berlin

For their project Kuhwatching, Buero fuer Gestaltung created a temporary rangeland with real cows in the middle of Berlin, Germany. The design group's aim was to illustrate the increasing estrangement between agriculture and consumers, and at the same time to trigger a simple joy for the viewer. During one weekend, the urban farm attracted over 3,000 guests to watch the four cows, Lothar, Tilda, Timm, and Tina.

Photos:
1 Stephan Vens, triggerhappyproductions;
2 Sebastian Donath

3

3 NEOZOON
Le Goût des Bêtes
Furcoat recycling, Paris.
Photo: NEOZOON

4 Mosstika
Hungarian Cattle Goes Green

4

NEOZOON
1 Cerfs

2 Renard

Photos: NEOZOON

1

Mosstika

Mosstika is the studio of Edina Tokodi and József Vályi-Tóth who first used handmade paper to create indoor sculptural installations and then expanded on this technique by incorporating live plant materials. This led to the idea of designing a series of gardens and public green spots around New York.

3 Rooster

2

3

4

4 PanoptICONS

Perceiving the increase of surveillance cameras in their city as a pest, Dutch artist duo Helden commented the development by placing urban birds with camera heads throughout the center of Utrecht.

Photo: Thomas voor 't Hekke

5

5, 6 Luzinterruptus Urban Nests

Colored birds placed in scaffolding joints in Madrid.

Photos: Gustavo Sanabria

6

EASY POUR

ANNA GARFORTH

Head Gardner
A family of totem heads with green hair-dos made from milk containers, created to watch over the city. Little did they know the city had its eyes on them. Most of the Head Gardners were purloined.

Photos: Anna Garforth

London-based artist Anna Garforth works with recycled and natural media. Her sustainable artworks have been used for public events, community projects, campaigns, publications, and exhibitions. With a strong background in design and illustration, her green fingers work moss into beautiful lettering, bark into animals, and rubbish into typographic art.

1

If this
is my day of harvest,
in what fields have I sown
my seeds?

2

3

1, 2 Prophet
The moss piece was written using Eleanor Steven's hand-written typeface. It was exhibited in Italy at the Rocca Paolina for the "Over Design Over" exhibition amongst 44 other internationally acclaimed artists. For the exhibition the artists chose a quote from Khalil Gibran's poem **The Prophet**: "If this is my day of harvest, in what fields have I sown my seeds?"

3 Watch Them Bloom

4, 5 Leaf Type

Eric Cheung & Sean Martindale
Public PARK(ing)
Photo: Sean Martindale

PARK(ing) Day

Park(ing) Day is an annual open-source global event where citizens, artists, and activists collaborate to temporarily transform metered parking spaces into Park(ing) spaces. Artist studio Rebar ignited the event with their first Park(ing) installation in San Francisco in 2005.
Photo: Andrea Scher/Rebar

Eric Cheung & Sean Martindale

Poster Pocket Plants

Planters made by finding and slicing into existing layers of illegally pasted poster advertisements in Toronto.

Photos: Sean Martindale

1

2

Posterchild
1, 2 ~~Flyer~~Planterboxes!

3 Mario Planter Boxes - 3D Versions

Photos: Posterchild

3

1

2

4

1 THE END.
Guerilla Gärtner
Photo: © Alva Unger

2, 3 Luzinterruptus
Packaged Vertical Garden
Photos: Gustavo Sanabria

4 Mosstika
Living Wall Installation

5-7 Eric Cheung &
Sean Martindale
Green P Pillar Planters
Photos: Sean Martindale

5

6

7

1

2

3

1, 2 Pete Dungey

Pothole Gardens

A series of public installations highlighting the problem of surface imperfections on Britain's roads.

Photos: © Pete Dungey

3 BACSAC

NL Architects
Moving Forest

Oliver Bishop-Young

Urban Plant Pot

Urban Plant Pot was one of a series of waste container conversions exploring alternative spaces to the existing urban environment. Due to the fact that most spaces are paved or tarmaced in urban environments it is hard to find places to grow plants. The design by Oliver Bishop addresses this unbalance giving people an allotment on their doorstep.

Photos: Tomas Valenzuela, © Oliver Bishop-Young

Studio Atuppertu

Urban Buds

Urban Buds is a concept for mobile vegetable garden units that can be placed in unused urban areas. The planter bags could be rented by city dwellers for cultivating food. Materials used for the bags are "Naturtherm" and "Recycletherm" produced by Manifattura Maiano. Those natural panels have the ability to keep the humidity inside the bags and favor the vertical growth of roots.

Photos: Shiro Inoue

Tattfoo Tan
Mobile Garden
Photo: Ensze Tan

1-800-44-SALEM

MOBILE
GARDEN

opposite page Tattfoo Tan

Mobile Garden

Mobile Garden is a do-it-yourself idea to repurpose found objects into a mobile planter to engage the public to be more sustainable and grow their own food, especially in the urban area.

Photos: Ensze Tan

Wildwuchs

To demonstrate for more biodiversity in the world, 100 people pushed 100 shopping carts filled with various species of plants through the streets of Kreuzberg district in Berlin.

Photos:
1 Marco Clausen;
2-4 Sabine Beyerle & David Reuter

1

2

3

4

1

4

2

3

Coloco
1-3 Bankside Birthday Barrows Parade
Wheelbarrow parade around parks and open spaces to celebrate the tenth birthdays of Tate Modern and Bankside Open Spaces Trust in London in 2010.
Photos: © Studio Public/ Benoît Lorent

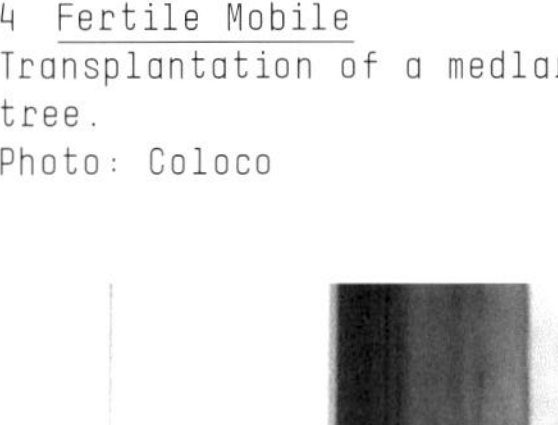

4 Fertile Mobile
Transplantation of a medlar tree.
Photo: Coloco

Alain Delorme
Totem #8
Photo: © Alain Delorme, courtesy Magda Danysz Gallery

INDEX

0–9

B

Fruit City
Vahakn Matossian
United Kingdom
www.FruitCity.co.uk
Pages 60, 61 Fruit City

FULGURO | Yves Fidalgo + Cédric Decroux
Switzerland
www.fulguro.ch
Page 100 reHOUSE/BATH
with Thomas Jomini Architecture Workshop
Page 101 Waternetworks Drops
Page 163 Green Shutter

Furnibloom
Iceland
www.furnibloom.com
Page 164 Regards from Iceland

Futurefarmers
Amy Franceschini, Michael Swaine
USA
www.futurefarmers.com
Page 40 Rainwater Harvester/Gray-water System Feedback Loop
Page 41 Nearest Nature; The Reverse Ark: Headlands Kitchen Garden

G

Garrett Finney
USA
crickettrailer.com
Page 143 Cricket Trailer

Ginza Farm Corp.
Kazuki Iimura
Japan
www.ginzanouen.jp
Page 54 Omotesandō Farm

Greenmeme
Freya Bardell, Brian Howe
USA
greenmeme.com
Page 163 Live Within Skin

Growing Power Inc.
USA
www.growingpower.org
Pages 16, 17 Growing Power

Guerrilla Gardening
Richard Reynolds and fellow guerrilla gardeners
United Kingdom
www.guerrillagardening.org
Page 200 Lavender Traffic Island

H

Haque Design + Research
South Korea
www.haque.co.uk
Pages 106, 107 Natural Fuse

Heatherwick Studio
United Kingdom
www.heatherwick.com
Pages 152, 153 UK Pavilion at the 2010 Shanghai Expo

Heidi Norton
USA
heidi-norton.com
Page 186 Channeling (Baby Spider Plants)

Helen Nodding
United Kingdom
storiesfromspace.co.uk
Page 114 Hideaway

Hoerr Schaudt Landscape Architects
USA
www.hoerrschaudt.com
Pages 50, 51 Gary Comer Youth Center Green Roof
with John Ronan Architects

I

i29
Netherlands
www.i29.nl
Page 149 Home 06

import.export Architecture
Oscar Rommens, Joris Van Reusel
Belgium
iea.be
Page 143 Urban Camping

Inclusive Studio
Raúl Goñi
Spain
inclusivestudio.com
Page 109 Pond

Innovo Design Co., Ltd.
China
www.innovo-design.com
Page 103 Green Trace

Itay Laniado
Israel
itay.designgroup.co.il
Page 37 Garden Tools

J

Janina Loeve
Netherlands
www.janinaloeve.nl
Page 176 Divers, Bouquets to Eat Alive

Jochem Faudet
United Kingdom
jochemfaudet.com
Page 93 Grow Your Own Greenhouse
Page 103 Freeloader

Joe Paine
South Africa
joepaine.withtank.com
Page 161 Kreep Planter

Juliette Warmenhoven
Netherlands
www.juliettewarmenhoven.nl
Page 89 Potato Music Box

Julio Radesca
Brazil
julioradesca.com
Page 104 Personal Fresh Air

K

Kabloom
Darren Wilson
United Kingdom
kabloom.co.uk
Pages 196, 197 Seedbom

Kai Linke
Germany
www.kailinke.com
Page 165 Roots

Kevin van Braak
Netherlands
www.kevinvanbraak.com
Page 145 Caravan 02

Kieren Jones
United Kingdom
www.kierenjones.com
Pages 134, 135 The Chicken Project

L

M

N

Omega Garden Int.
Ted Marchildon
Canada
www.omegagarden.com
Pages 94, 95 Omega Garden

Owl Project
United Kingdom
owlproject.com
Page 168 Log1k

P

Pam & Jenny
Belgium
pametjenny.be
Page 39 Euralille-Parc des Dondaines
with Nathalie Pollet

PanoptICONS
Helden
Netherlands
www.panopticons.nl
Page 207 PanoptICONS

PARK(ing) Day
Rebar
USA
www.parkingday.org
Page 213 PARK(ing)

Patrick Blanc
France
www.verticalgardenpatrickblanc.com
Page 120 Mur Végétal
Page 149 Centre Commercial, Les Passages, Boulogne-Billancourt

Paul Loebach
USA
www.paulloebach.com
Page 168 Great Camp Collection

Pete Dungey
United Kingdom
www.petedungey.com
Page 218 Pothole Gardens

Philips Design
Netherlands
www.design.philips.com
Page 86 Philips Design Food Probe: Biosphere Home Farm

PostCarden
Aimée Furnival
United Kingdom
www.postcarden.com
Page 93 PostCarden
by Another Studio for Design

Posterchild
Canada
www.bladediary.com
Page 215 ~~Flyer~~Planterboxes!; Mario Planter Boxes - 3D Versions

Pour les Alpes
Annina Gähwiler, Tina Stieger
Switzerland
www.pourlesalpes.ch
Page 160 Crystal "Chapütschin"

Prinzessinnengärten
Germany
www.prinzessinnengarten.net
Pages 10-13 Prinzessinnen-gärten

Pushak AS
Norway
www.pushak.no
Pages 146, 147 Moss Your City

R

Renzo Piano
Italy
www.rpbw.com
Pages 44, 45 California Academy of Sciences

ROA
Belgium
www.ROA-bestiaria.com
Page 202 Squirrel Williamsburg; No title; Lenticular Rabbit

Rogier Martens
Netherlands
rogiermartens.nl
Page 140 Build-It-Yourself Treehouse (De Zelfbouwboomhut)
with Sam Van Veluw

ryan lingard design, llc
USA
www.rlingard.com
Page 140 Signal Shed

Ryan Rhodes
USA
www.biggerthangiants.com
Page 59 Johnson's Backyard Garden Corporate Design

Sandrine Estrade Boulet
France
sandrine-estrade-boulet.com
Page 201 Pom-Pom Girl

Scheltens & Abbenes Studio
Netherlands
www.scheltens-abbenes.com
Page 193 Bouquet IX

Sebastian Errazuriz
USA
www.meetsebastian.com
Page 203 The Day Cows Fly

Shinji Turner-Yamamoto
Japan/USA
yamamotoshinji.net;
globaltreeproject.org
Pages 170, 171 Global Tree Project: Hanging Garden

Sophia Martineck
Germany
www.martineck.com/
Page 92 Greenhouse

Specimen Editions
Constance Guisset
France
specimen-editions.fr
Page 89 Duplex

Stedelijk Museum Amsterdam, Marjetica Potrc, Wilde Westen
Netherlands
www.stedelijk.nl
Page 36 The Cook, the Farmer, His Wife and Their Neighbor

Steven Burke
France
stevenburke.org
Page 169 Poor Little Trees

String Gardens
Fedor van der Valk
Netherlands
stringgardens.com
Pages 172, 173 String Gardens

Studio Atuppertu
Gionata Gatto
Netherlands
www.atuppertu.com
Page 222 Urban Buds

Studio Formafantasma
Netherlands
www.formafantasma.com
Pages 66, 67 Autarchy

Studio Gorm
John Arndt, Wonhee Jeong
USA
www.studiogorm.com
Page 83 Flow2

Studio Job
Job Smeets, Nynke Tynagel
Belgium
www.studiojob.be
Pages 150, 151 Bavaria collection: Moss, NY, exhibited: Design Miami, Miami; Studio Job Gallery, Antwerp

Studio Makkink & Bey
Netherlands
www.studiomakkinkbey.nl
Pages 98, 99 The Bell Garden
Page 166 Gardening Bench; Tree Trunk Bench
Page 167 Sandbench Bulldozer

Studio Toogood
United Kingdom
www.studiotoogood.com
Pages 68, 69 Corn Craft
Pages 70, 71 Super Natural

Studio Weave
United Kingdom
www.studioweave.com
Page 140 Freya's Cabin

Studiomama
Nina Tolstrup
United Kingdom
www.studiomama.com
Page 82 The Mobile Outdoor Kitchen
Page 133 Bird Frame

T

Tattfoo Tan
USA
www.tattfoo.com
Pages 223, 224 Mobile Garden

THE END.
Alva Unger
Austria
www.theend.at
Page 197 Guerilla Gärtner
Page 216 Guerilla Gärtner

The Grand Daddy
South Africa
granddaddy.co.za
Page 144 Airstream Penthouse Trailer Park

The Union Street Urban Orchard
United Kingdom
www.unionstreetorchard.org.uk; www.architecturefoundation.org.uk
Pages 6-9 The Union Street Urban Orchard

Tjep.
Netherlands
www.tjep.com
Page 128 Oogst 1
Page 129 Oogst 1000; Amsterdam City Garden

Tony Minh Nguyen
USA
www.minh-t.com
Page 197 Flower Grenade

Triptyque
Brazil
www.triptyque.com
Page 117 Harmonia 57

Turf Design
Australia
www.turfdesign.com
Pages 62, 63 Salad Bar
with Taylor Thomson Whitting, Elmich Australia, Andreasens Green, Lynda Roberts, Bailey's Joinery, RPS Contracting

Tuur Van Balen
United Kingdom
www.tuurvanbalen.com
Pages 136, 137 Pigeon d'Or
Funded by the Flemish Authorities' Agency for the Arts.

U

UP Projects
United Kingdom
upprojects.com
Page 79 Mobile Picnic Pavilion
by Francis Thorburn
Page 132 Spontaneous City in the Tree of Heaven
by London Fieldworks

V

Vanessa Harden
United Kingdom
www.vanessaharden.com
Pages 198, 199 The Subversive Gardener

Victory Gardens
USA
www.sfvictorygardens.org
Page 38 Victory Gardens

Virginia Echeverria Whipple
Chile
virginiaecheverria.com
Page 43 Untitled

What if: projects Ltd.
United Kingdom
what-if.info
Page 14 Vacant Lot
Developed in partnership with Groundworks London.

Wildwuchs
Beyreut (Sabine Beyerle, David Reuter)
Germany
web.me.com/davidreuter/Biodiversität/home.html
Page 225 Wildwuchs

Windowfarms
Britta Riley
USA
windowfarms.org
Page 97 Windowfarms
in cooperation with all 15,000+ memebers at our.windowfarms.org

woollypocket
Miguel Nelson
USA
www.woollypocket.com
Page 162 woollypocket

WORK Architecture Company
USA
www.work.ac
Pages 22-24 Public Farm 1
Pages 126, 127 Locavore Fantasia; Plug Out

ZENDOME.ecopod
Nicola Meekin, Jim Milligan
United Kingdom
domesweetdome.co.uk
Page 142 Ecopod
with Designers Anonymous

MY GREEN CITY

Back to Nature with Attitude and Style

Edited by Robert Klanten, Sven Ehmann, and Kitty Bolhöfer
Texts by Kitty Bolhöfer

Cover by Jonas Herfurth for Gestalten
Cover photography (top to bottom) by Alain Delorme, Shiinoki Shunsuke, Anne Hamersky, Brooklyn Grange, Mike Massaro, Philips Design – Food Probes, Sandrine Estrade Boulet
Cover illustration by Sophia Martineck
Layout by Jonas Herfurth for Gestalten
Typefaces: Lisbon by Monotype Imaging; Clarendon by Linotype; T-Star Mono Round by Mika Mischler, Foundry: www.gestalten.com/fonts

Project management by Elisabeth Honerla for Gestalten
Project management assistance by Vanessa Diehl for Gestalten
Production management by Janine Milstrey for Gestalten
Proofreading by Bettina Klein
Printed by Livonia, Made in Europe

Published by Gestalten, Berlin 2011
ISBN 978-3-89955-334-5

For more information, please visit www.gestalten.com

Bibliographic information published by the Deutsche Nationalbibliothek.
The Deutsche Nationalbibliothek lists this publication in the Deutsche Nationalbibliografie; detailed bibliographic data is available online at http://dnb.d-nb.de.

None of the content in this book was published in exchange for payment by commercial parties or designers; Gestalten selected all included work based solely on its artistic merit.

This book was printed according to the internationally accepted FSC and ISO 14001 standards for environmental protection, which specify requirements for an environmental management system.

Gestalten is a climate-neutral company and so are our products. We collaborate with the non-profit carbon offset provider myclimate (www.myclimate.org) to neutralize the company's carbon footprint produced through our worldwide business activities by investing in projects that reduce CO_2 emissions (www.gestalten.com/myclimate).

Page 60 Fruit City

Page 194 Seed Packets

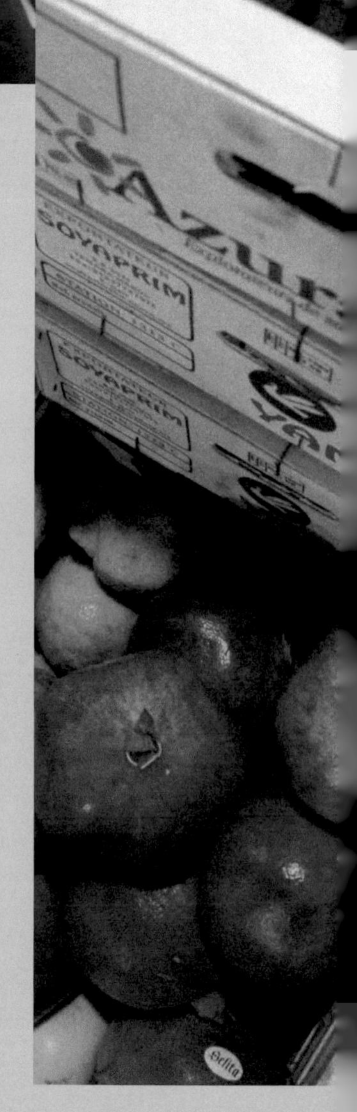

Page 59 Johnson's Backyard Garden Corporate Design

Page 17 Growing Power

Page 13 Prinzessinnengärten

Page 73 BQ Interactive Dinner

Page 24 Public Farm 1

Page 160 Crystal "Chapütschin"

Page 39 Euralille

Page 182 Psychocandy

Page 149 Home 06

Page 217 Packaged Vertical Garden

Page 71 Super Natural

Page 162 woollypocket

Page 8 The Union Street Urban Orchard